First Edition
Genuine Autographed Collectible

____

Do you want me to sign it in ink or in lipstick?

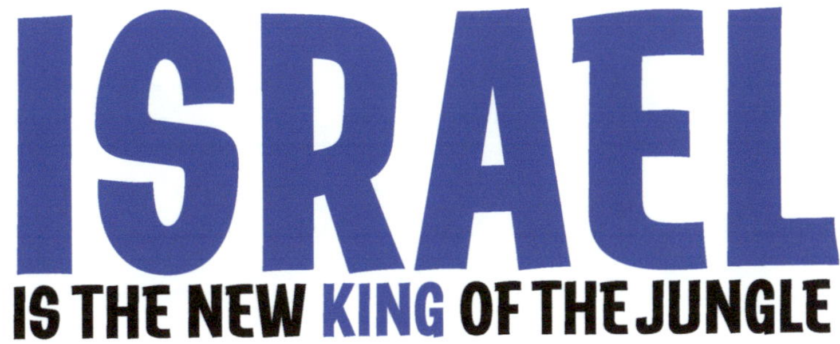

Gift Card

Date:

To:

From:

Message:

ISRAEL IS THE NEW KING OF THE JUNGLE

KADIMAH PRESS
GIFTS OF GENIUS

Books may be purchased for education, business, or sales promotional use.
ISBN Hardcover: 979-8-3485-5324-1
ISBN Paperback: 979-8-3485-5324-1
ISBN e-book: 979-8-3485-5326-5
Library of Congress Control Number: 2025903527

FAN MAIL:
SharonEstherLampert.com
FANS@SharonEstherLampert.com

Cover and Interior Book Design: Creative Genius Sharon Esther Lampert
Editor: Dave Segal

Palm Beach Book Publisher, Phone: 917-767-5843
Sharon@PalmBeachBookPublisher.com
To Order Book:
Ingram, 1 Ingram Blvd. La Vergne, TN 37086-3629
Phone: 615-793-5000
Fax orders: 615-287-6990

First Edition

Manufactured in the United States of America

ISRAEL

IS THE NEW KING OF THE JUNGLE

Every Thought In Your Head Was Put There By a Writer!

Sharon Esther Lampert

DEDICATION

MOMMY

LOVE OF MY LIFETIME

WHO KNEW WHO I WAS FROM THE INSIDE OUT

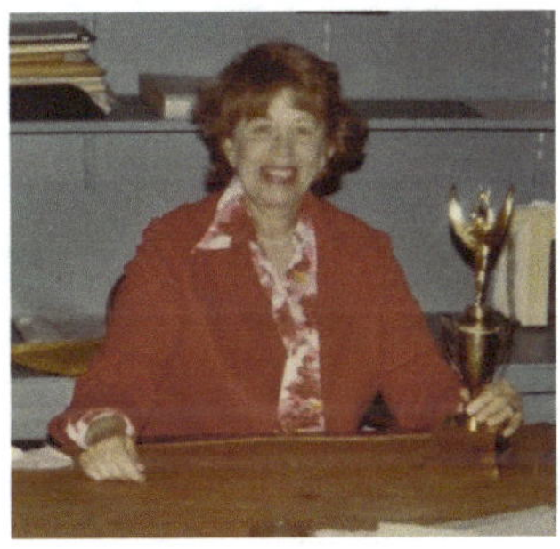

Age 9
THE QUEEN HAS ARRIVED!
My daughter is a poet,
philosopher, and teacher.
She is the Princess & Pea!
BEAUTY & BRAINS!
LOVE & XOXO
MOMMY

What Do Books Do?
BOOKS ARE POWERFUL

Books Educate!
Books Enlighten!
Books Empower!
Books Emancipate!
Books Entertain!
Books Spring Eternal!
Books Drive Exploration!
Books Spark Evolution!
Books Ignite Revolution!

Sharon Esther Lampert

“I began my social
media posts after
October 7, 2023,
and my posts were
“MOST RELEVANT.”
Israelis reached out
to use them, and
thanked me. I made
a valuable contribution!

Sharon Esther Lampert

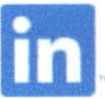

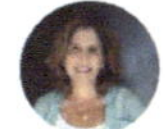

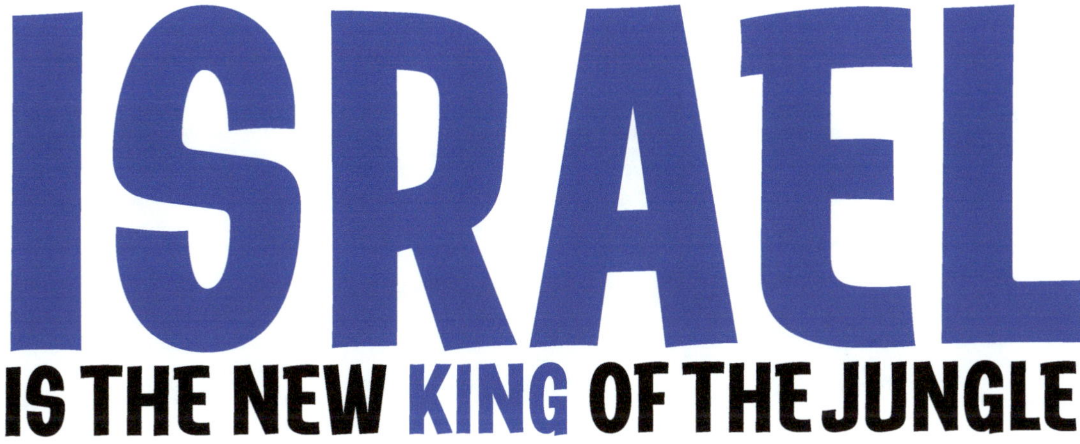

Debi Burrow replied to your comment

"Thank you for providing all this info. It's good to know the facts
instead of just opinions. "

Barak Finkelshtein mentioned you in a comment

"Thank you Sharon Lampert M.A., M.A. for your clear and factual
breakdown of the situation in Israel. Your comment is a..."

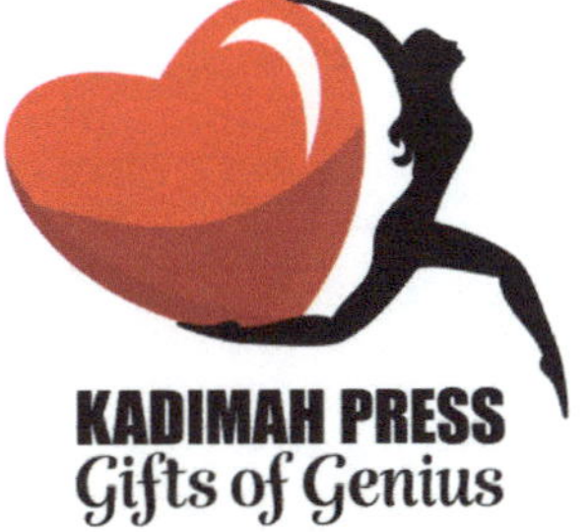

LITERATURE IS POWERFUL BEYOND WORDS FOR IT CREATES WORLDS

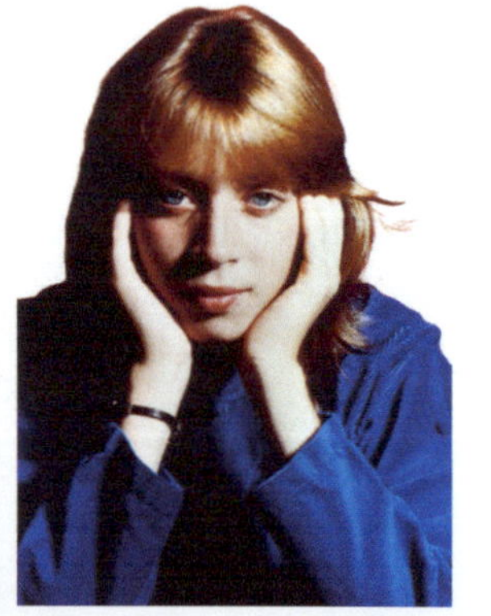

Sharon Esther Lampert

Table of Contents

WORLD FAMOUS JEWISH QUOTES

1. **ISRAEL IS THE NEW KING OF THE JUNGLE**
2. Israel Has 13 Nobel Prizes
3. **THE DELIVERERS**
4. **JEWS: THE CHOSEN PEOPLE**
5. Wherever Jews Go, Grass Grows; Wherever Israelis Go, Gardens Grow
6. If You Will It, It Is No Dream
7. One Mitzvah Can change the World, Two Will Make You Tired
8. **TIKKUN OLAM**
9. **KING BIBI** Is the Greatest World Leader Since the Dawn of History - 2 Designs
10. There Are 5 Books of Moses & 5 Million Books of Jewish Comedy
11. When You're Jewish, There Is No Such Thing As Too Much Drama
12. RECONSERVADOX
13. BORN JEWISH
14. I AM a PROPHET
15. GOD IS GO! DO!
16. **BEZALEL: EXODUS 31:3**
17. 8 HOURS
18. Artist Abraham Lampert

A
WRITER
IS AN
ARTIST
WHO PAINTS WITH
WORDS
Sharon Esther Lampert

Table of Contents

OCTOBER 7TH WORLD FAMOUS QUOTES

1. Every Story Is the Same Story: Cain and Abel
2. **INNOVATION NATION**
3. **LET MY PEOPLE GO!**
4. ANTI-SEMITISM
5. Genesis: 1.2 **TOHU VAVOHU**
6. YOU CANNOT NEGOTIATE WTH EVIL
7. Jews Live and Die According to God's Divine Plan
8. Jews Are the Happiest People on Planet Earth
9. Israel Has the Right Friends
10. **FREE ARABS**
11. **IRAN: NOW OR NEVER!**
12. 18 Years
13. GOD Speaks in Whispers
14. Hamas Took the Whole World Hostage
15. Entire Countries Hijacked by Terrorists
16. 36 Years
17. Oct 7: Africa
18. Broken World of Broken People
19. Food Truck
20. Terrorists Always Have the Advantage - Play Them Or Get Played By Them!
21. Florida Rodents and GAZA Terrorists
22. ICE
23. Know Nothings
24. OBSESSION
25. Paradign Shift 1. Offense Over Defense!
26. Paradign Shift 2. Take No Prisoners!
27. Paradign Shift 3. Build the Third Temple
28. Paradign Shift 4. Take Control of Education System
29. Paradign Shift 5. University of Democracy
30. Bigger Than Any Bible Story!

What Is Art?

Art is the expression of the
soul of a human being.
When art moves you,
one soul has reached out
to touch another.

SHARON ESTHER LAMPERT
PRODIGY, PROPHET, PHILOSOPHER, POET
PEACEMAKER, PHOTON SUPERHERO, PINUP

SEE THE WORLD
THROUGH THE EYES
OF A CREATIVE GENIUS

Table of Contents

WORLD FAMOUS QUOTES

1. Every Thought In Your Head Was Put There By A Writer
2. What Do Books Do?
3. Literature is More Powerful Than Words For it Creates Worlds
4. Writer: An Artist Who Paints with Words
5. What Is Art?
6. BE ART
7. FIGHT TO LIVE, LIVE TO FIGHT, BORN TO DIE
8. WORLD PEACE EQUATION
9. No Fakes! No Flops! No Filler! No Fluff! No Fudge! No Fat! No F-Bomb!
10. **TRUE LOVE**
11. Do You Want Me to Sign it in Ink or in Lipstick?
12. Solve Just One Problem **EDUCATION** Save the Entire World
13. **ONE GLOBAL ENEMY: IGNORANCE**
14. **GOD IS GO! DO!**
15. The First Step in Education Last a Lifetime
16. All Writers Write the Exact Same Way
17. **WARNING PRODIGY**
18. My Books Are My Remains Handle Them Gently
19. THE 22 COMMANDMENTS: YOU HAD TO OUTDO MOSES!

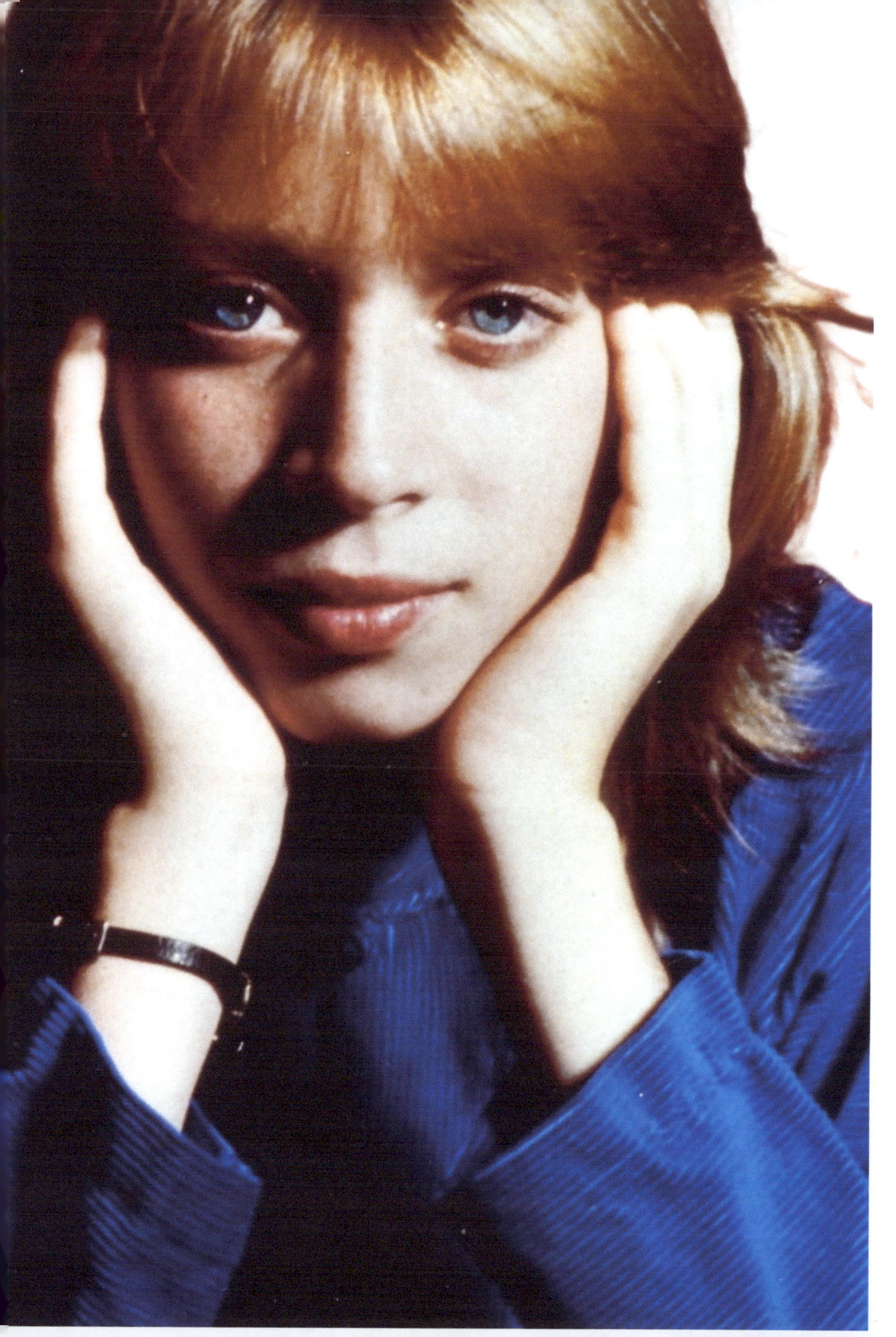

ISRAEL
Is The
New
KING
of The
Jungle
Sharon Esther Lampert
PRINCESS KADIMAH
8TH PROPHETESS OF ISRAEL
AM YISRAEL CHAI

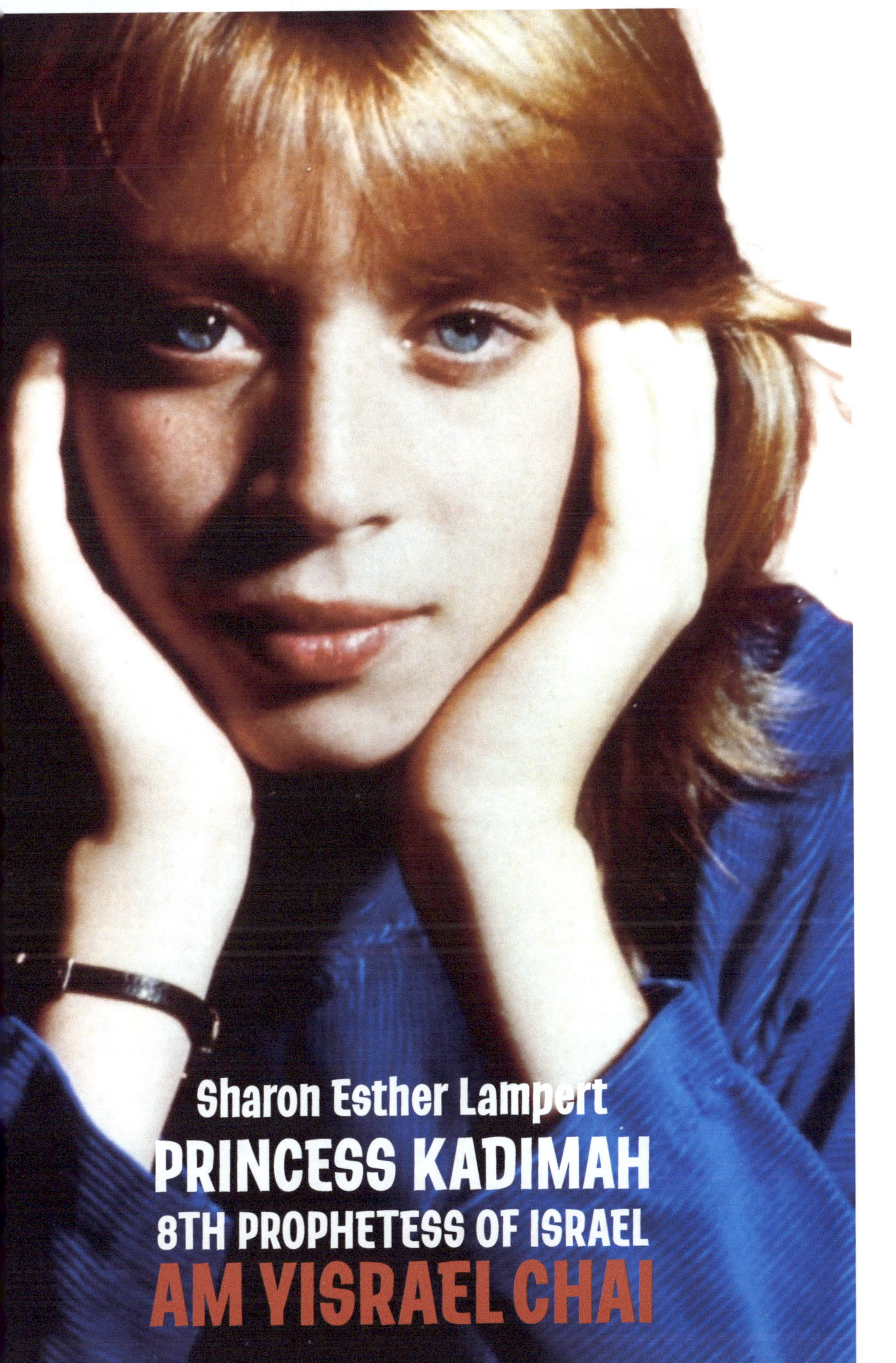

JEWS: THE CHOSEN PEOPLE

Jews Earned 22% of the World's Nobel Prizes that Benefit All Humanity!

Israel Has 13 Nobel Prizes!

Jews Are 0.2 Percent
of the World's Population
54 Percent of the
World Chess Champions
27 Percent of the
Nobel Physics Laureates
31 Percent of the
Medicine Laureates
21 Percent of the
Ivy League Student Bodies
26 Percent of the
Kennedy Center Honorees
37 Percent of the Academy
Award-Winning Directors
38 Percent of Leading Philanthropists
51 Percent of the Pulitzer Prize
Winners for Nonfiction

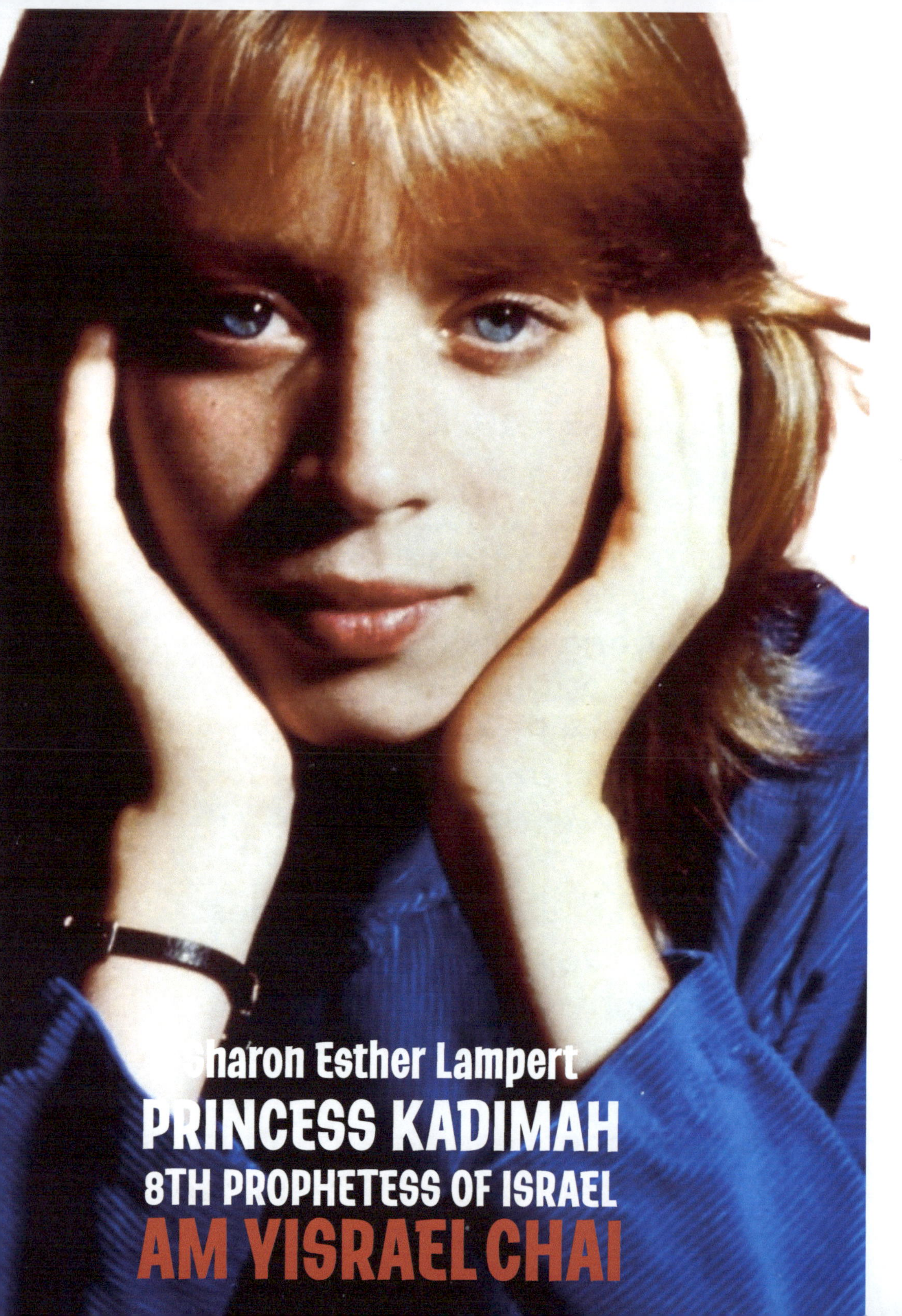

THE DELIVERERS

MOSES
THE PROMISED LAND

ISRAEL DEFENSE FORCES
VICTORIES OF JOSHUA

KING DAVID
CAPITAL OF JERUSALEM

KING SOLOMON
THE FIRST TEMPLE

THEODORE HERZL
ZIONISM

DAVID BEN-GURION
STATE OF ISRAEL

BENJAMIN NETANYAHU
INNOVATION NATION

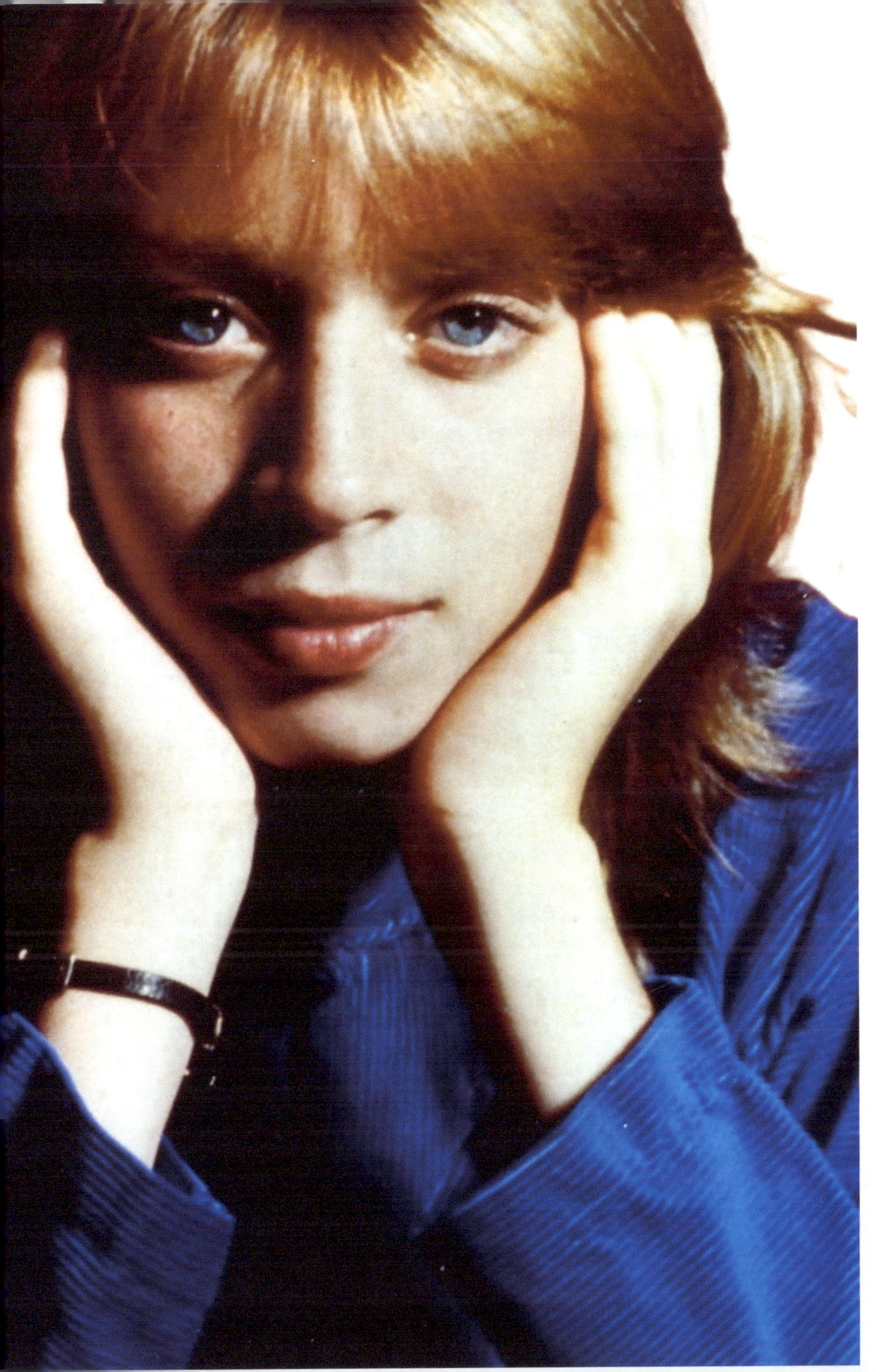

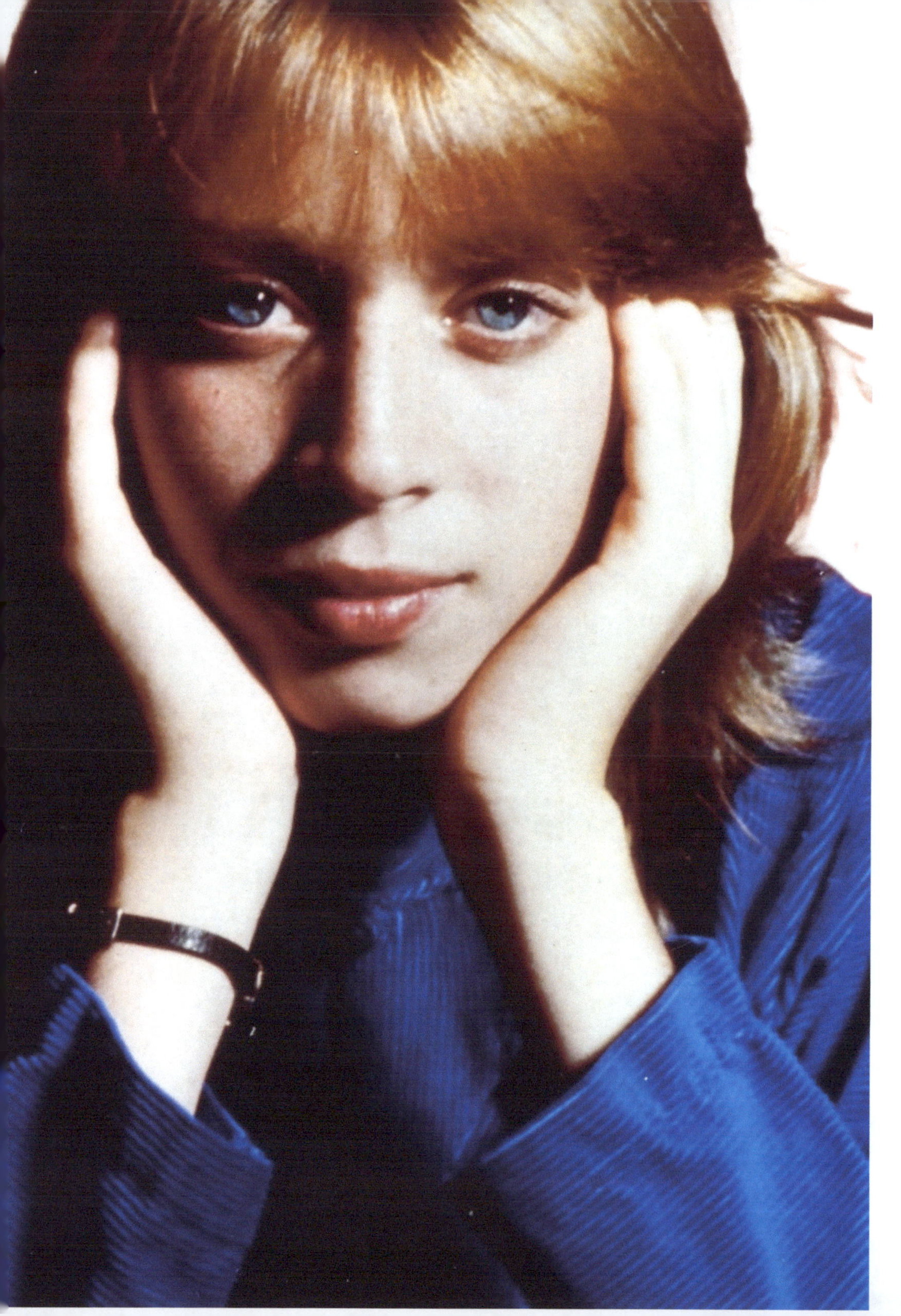

Wherever Jews Go,
Grass Grows
Wherever Israelis Go,
Gardens Grow

Sharon Esther Lampert
PRINCESS KADIMAH
8TH PROPHETESS OF ISRAEL
AM YISRAEL CHAI

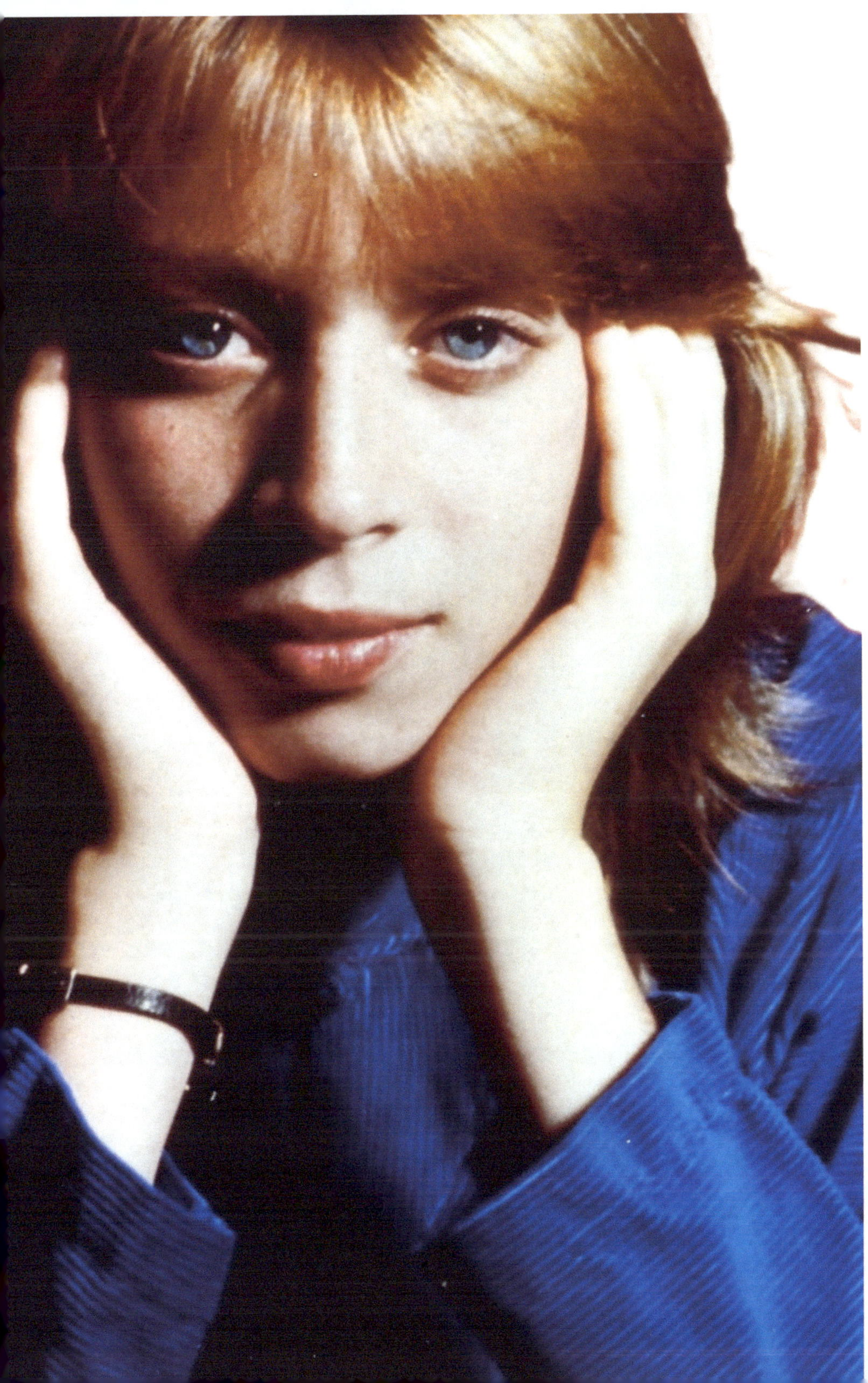

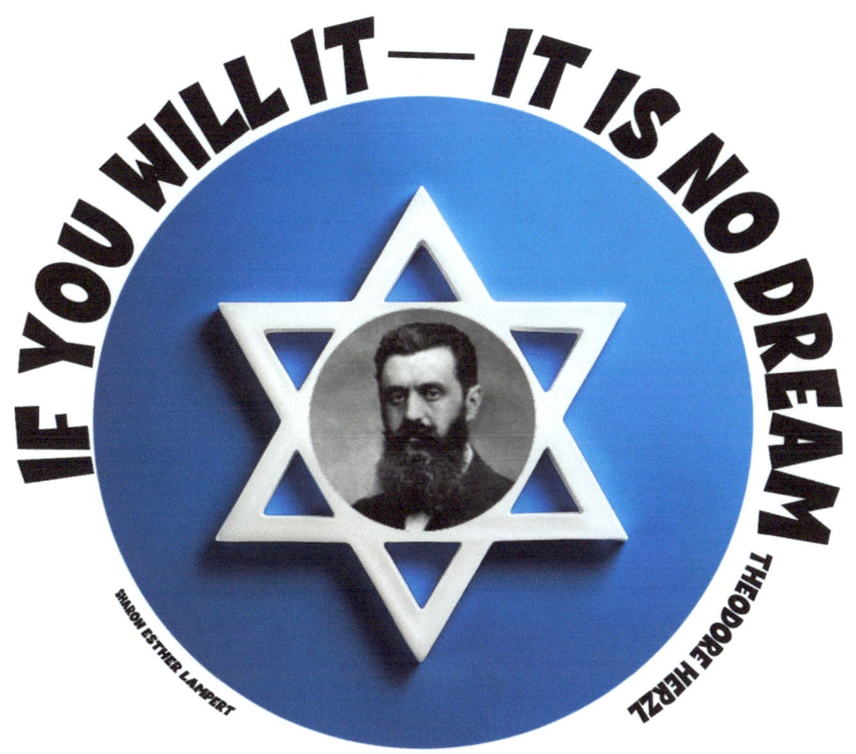

Sharon Esther Lampert
PRINCESS KADIMAH
8TH PROPHETESS OF ISRAEL
AM YISRAEL CHAI

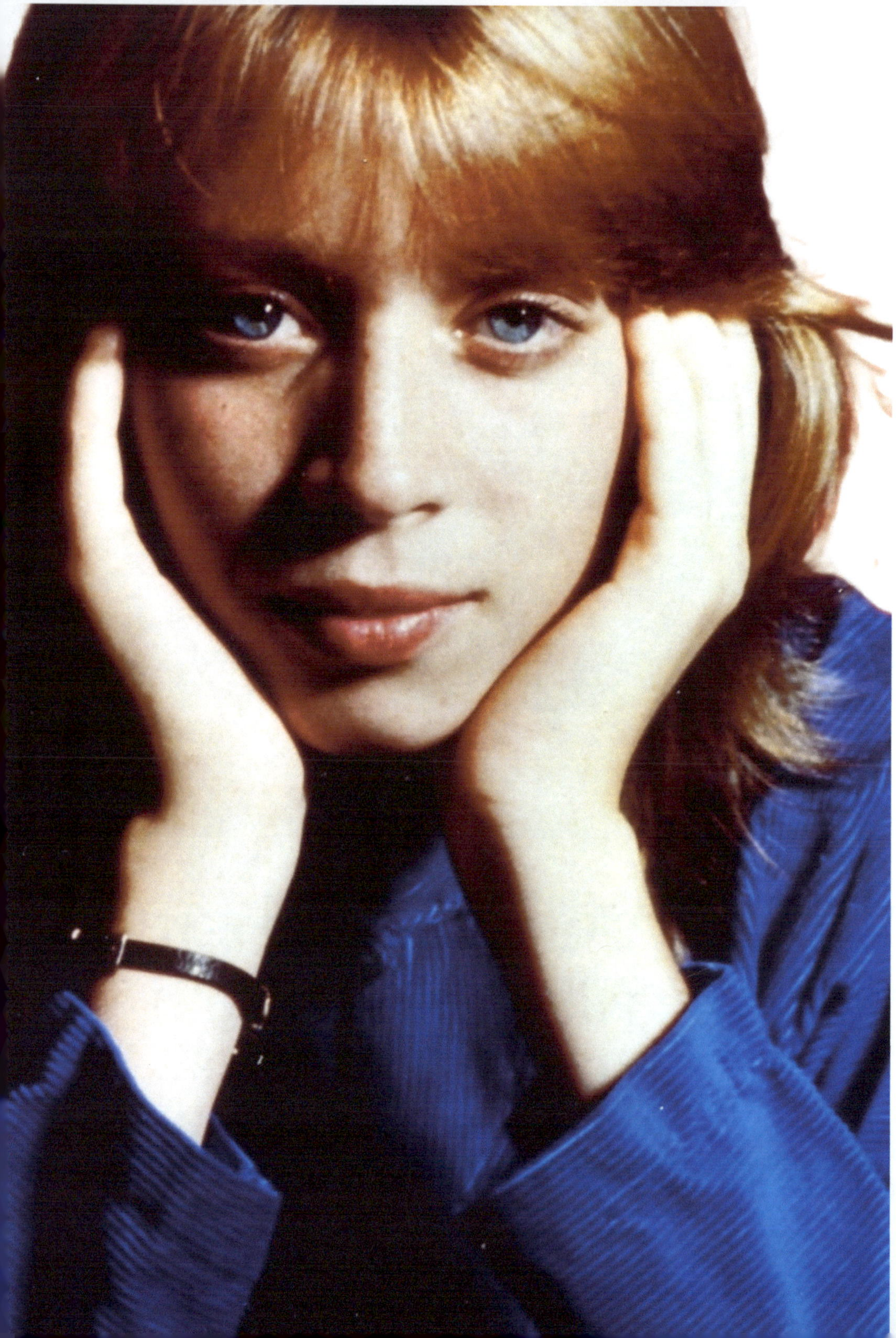

One Mitzvah Can Change The World Two Will Make You Tired

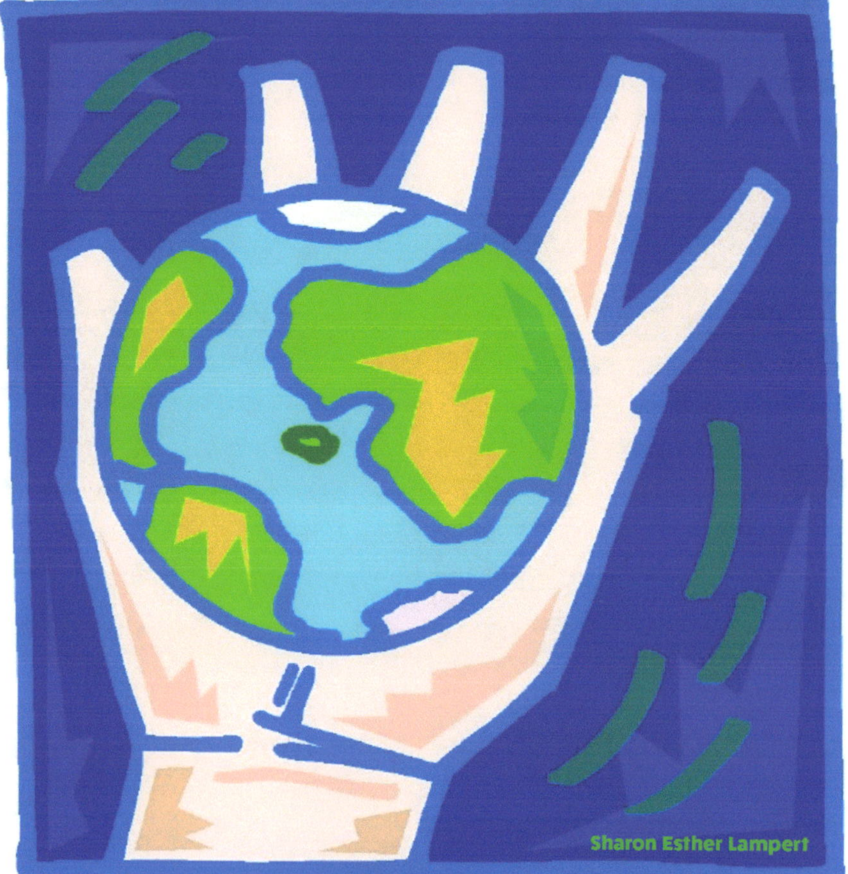

Sharon Esther Lampert
PRINCESS KADIMAH
8TH PROPHETESS OF ISRAEL
AM YISRAEL CHAI

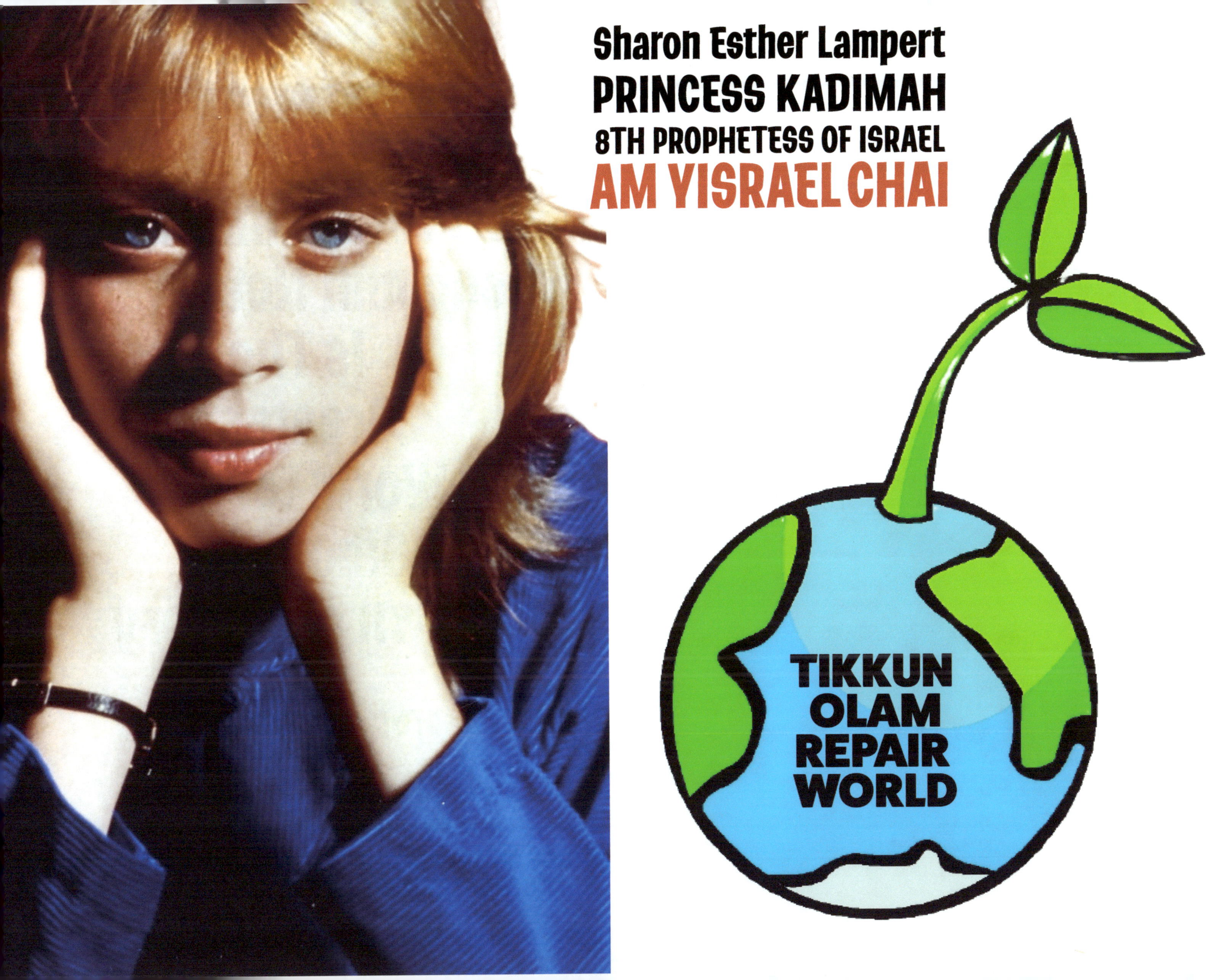

Sharon Esther Lampert
PRINCESS KADIMAH
8TH PROPHETESS OF ISRAEL
AM YISRAEL CHAI
TIKKUN OLAM REPAIR WORLD

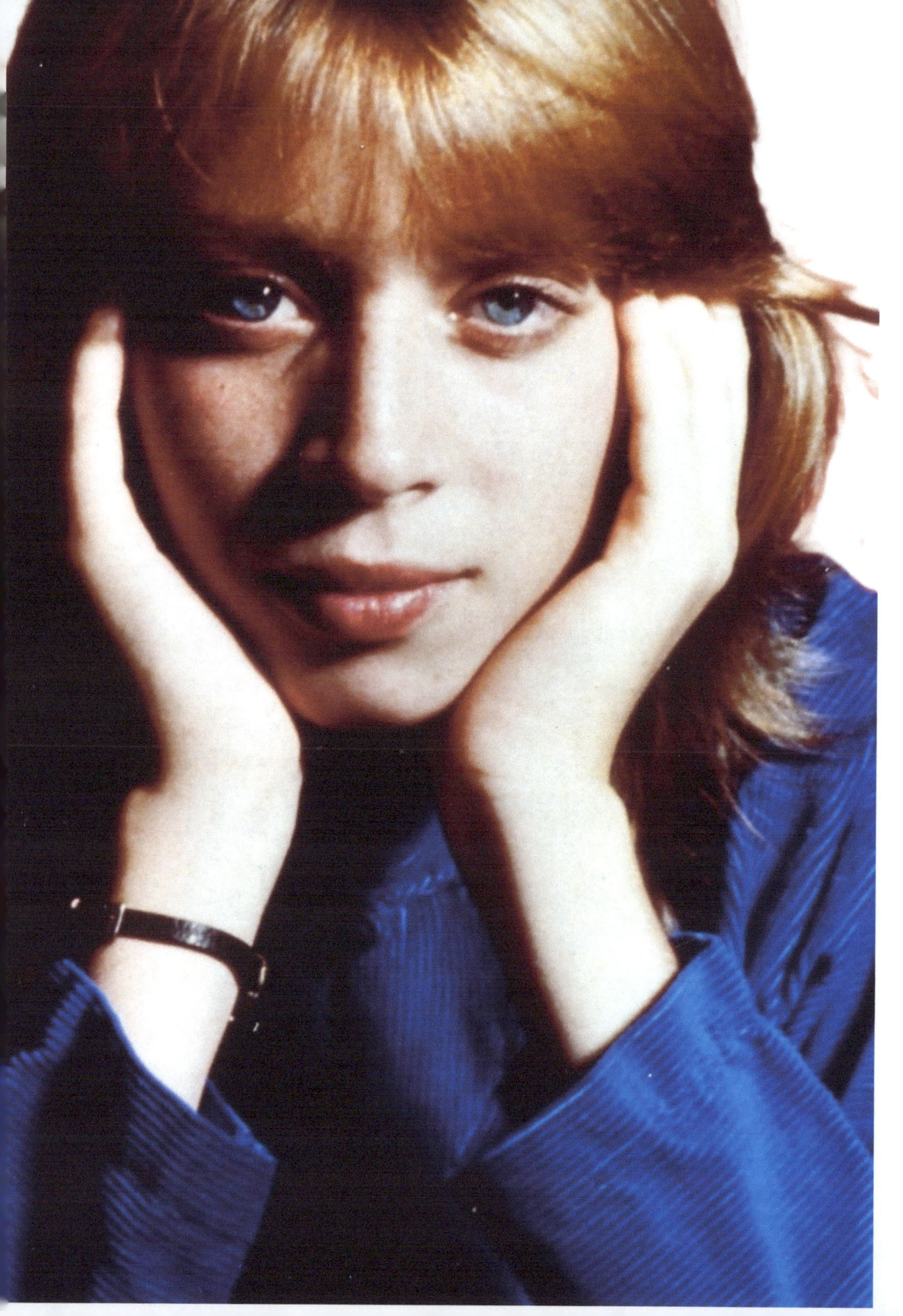

KING BIBI
Prime Minister
Benjamin Netanyahu
Is The
Greatest
World Leader
Since The
Dawn of History

Sharon Esther Lampert
PRINCESS KADIMAH
8TH PROPHETESS OF ISRAEL
AM YISRAEL CHAI

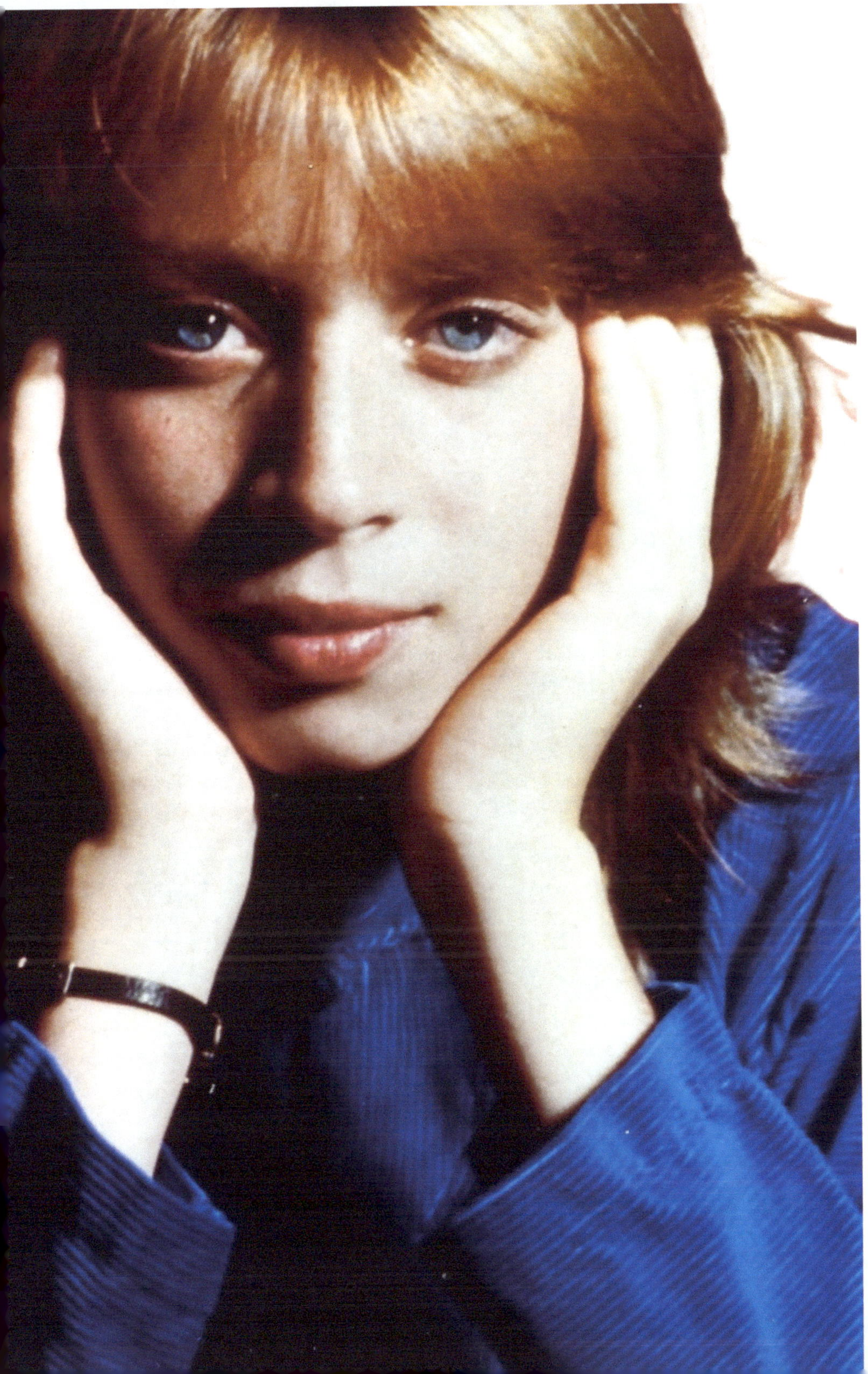

INNOVATION NATION
KING BIBI

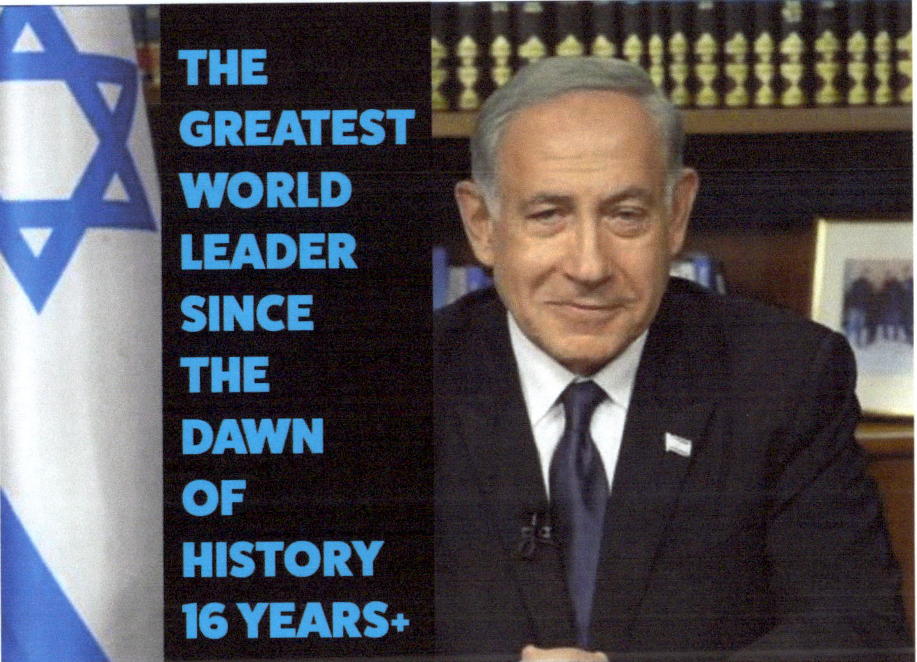

Sharon Esther Lampert
PRINCESS KADIMAH
8TH PROPHETESS OF ISRAEL
AM YISRAEL CHAI

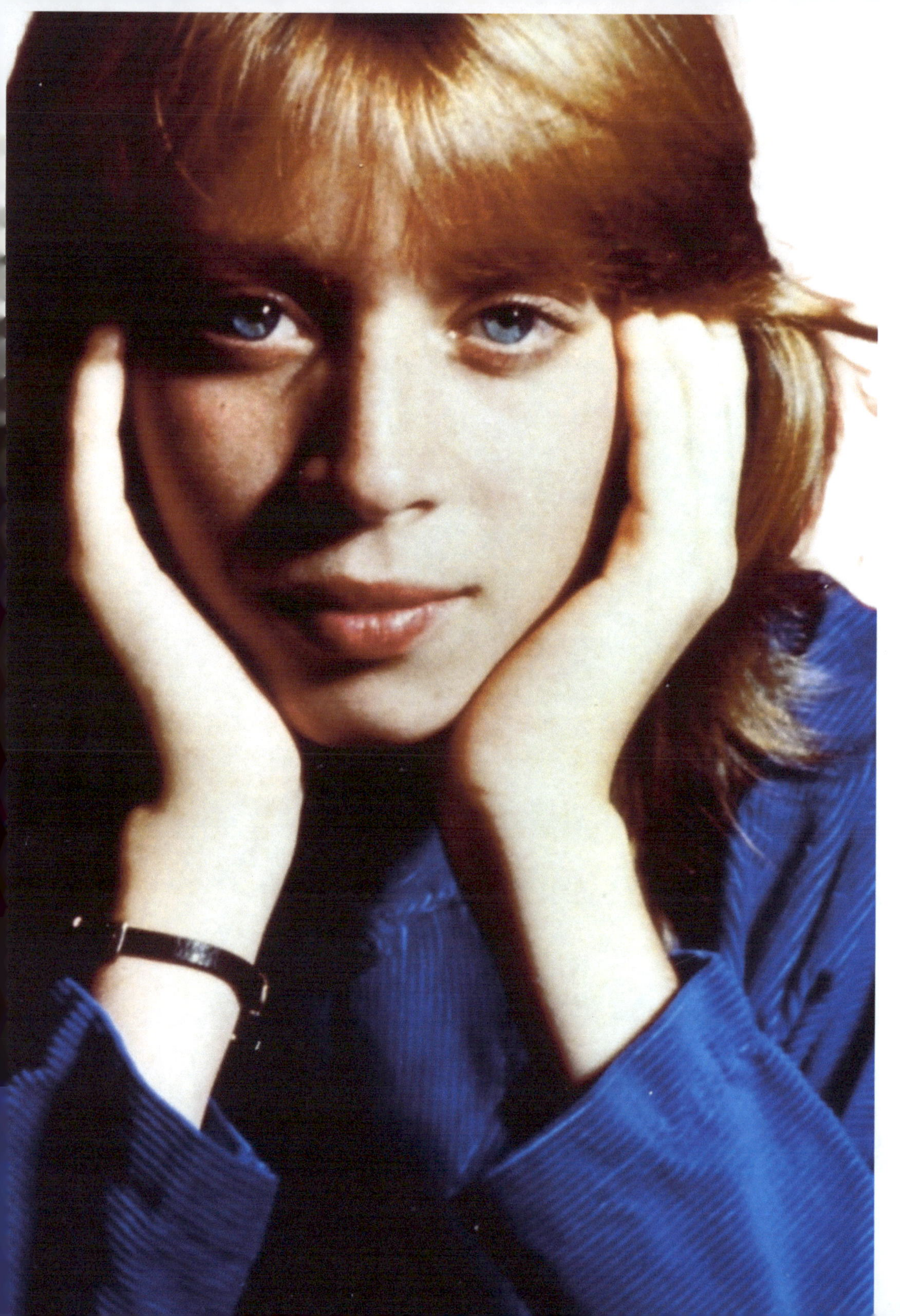

There Are 5 Books of

MOSES

and 5 Million Books of

JEWISH COMEDY

Sharon Esther Lampert

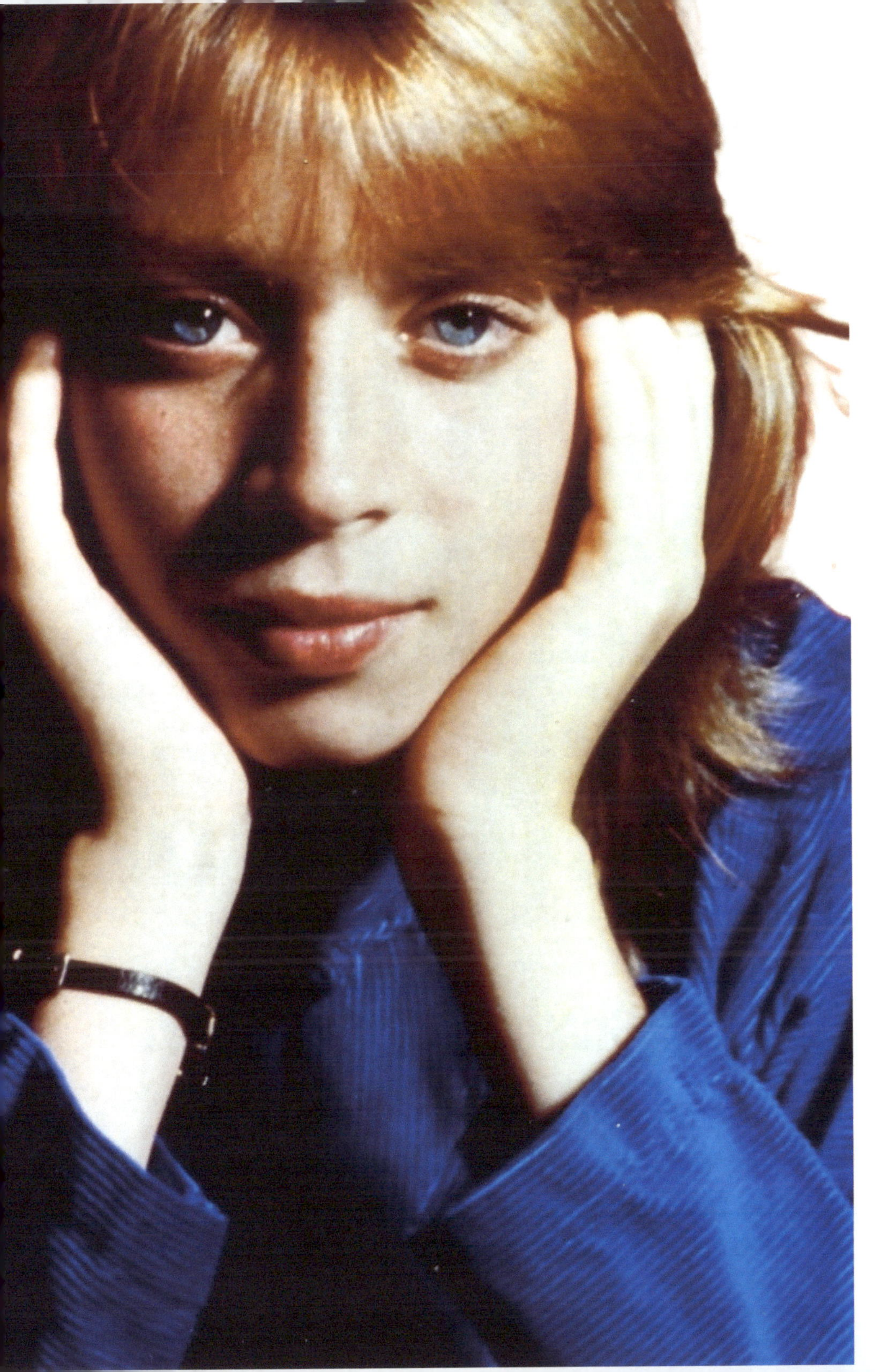

When You're JEWISH There Is No Such Thing As Too Much Drama

Sharon Esther Lampert
PRINCESS KADIMAH
8TH PROPHETESS OF ISRAEL
AM YISRAEL CHAI

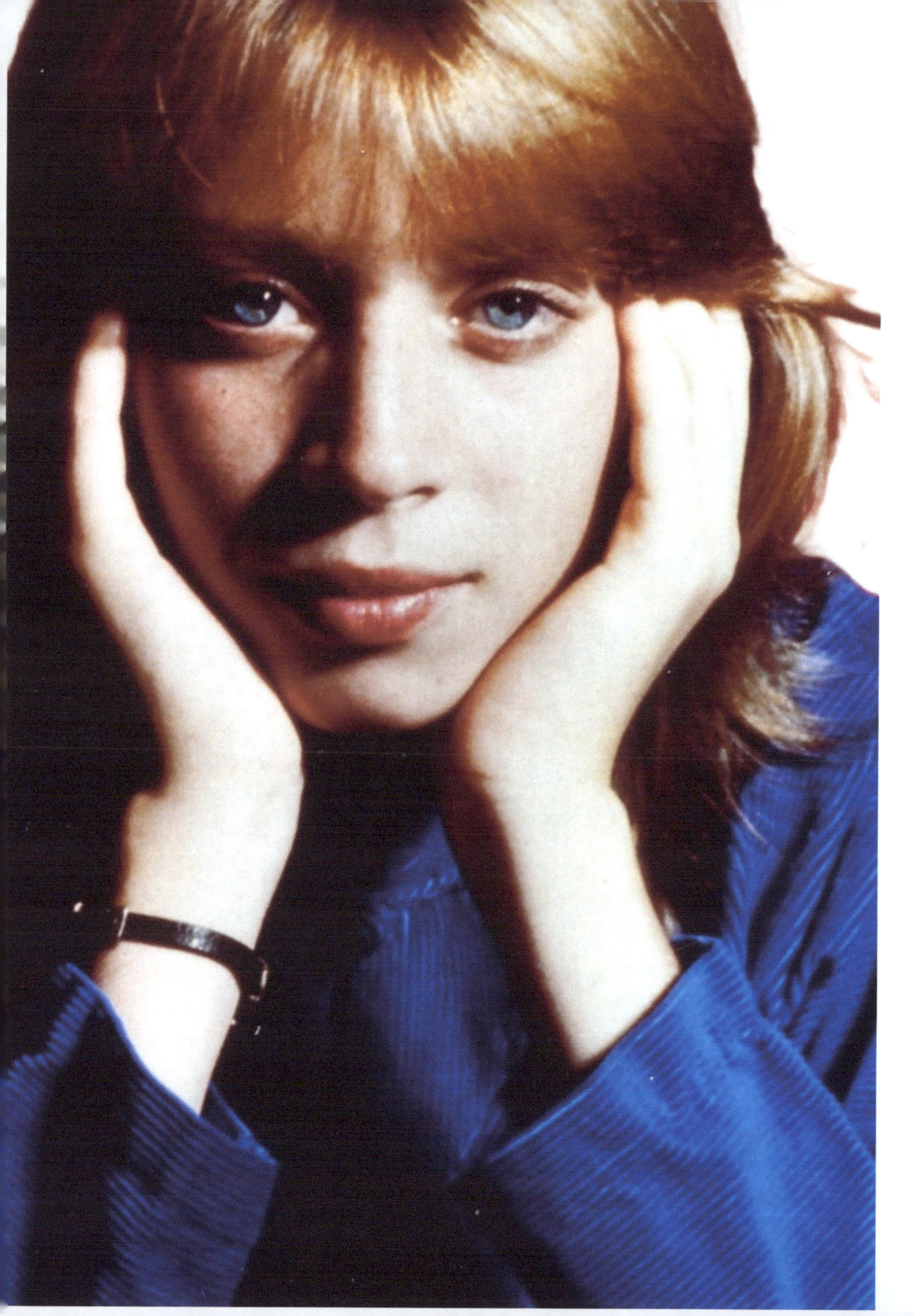

Every Story Is the Same Story:
CAIN & ABEL

Sharon Esther Lampert
PRINCESS KADIMAH
8TH PROPHETESS OF ISRAEL
AM YISRAEL CHAI

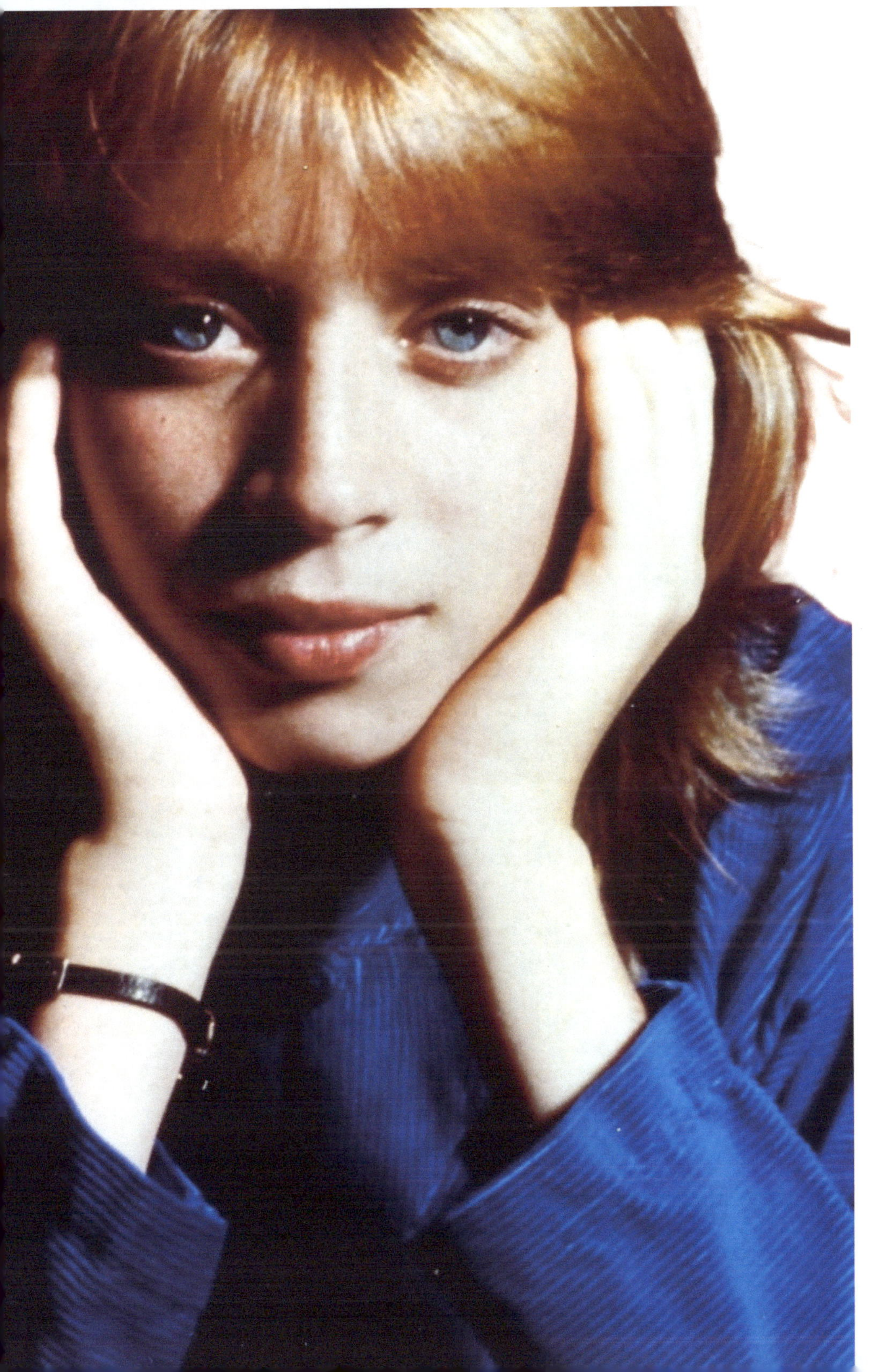

"After the Holocaust of
6 Million Jewish Lives Lost,
We Rebuilt Our
3000-Year-Old
Ancestral Homeland into

INNOVATION NATION

After Oct 7TH,
We Had the Power to
Destroy Our Enemies
Not Be Destroyed
By Our Enemies."

Sharon Esther Lampert
PRINCESS KADIMAH
8TH PROPHETESS OF ISRAEL
AM YISRAEL CHAI

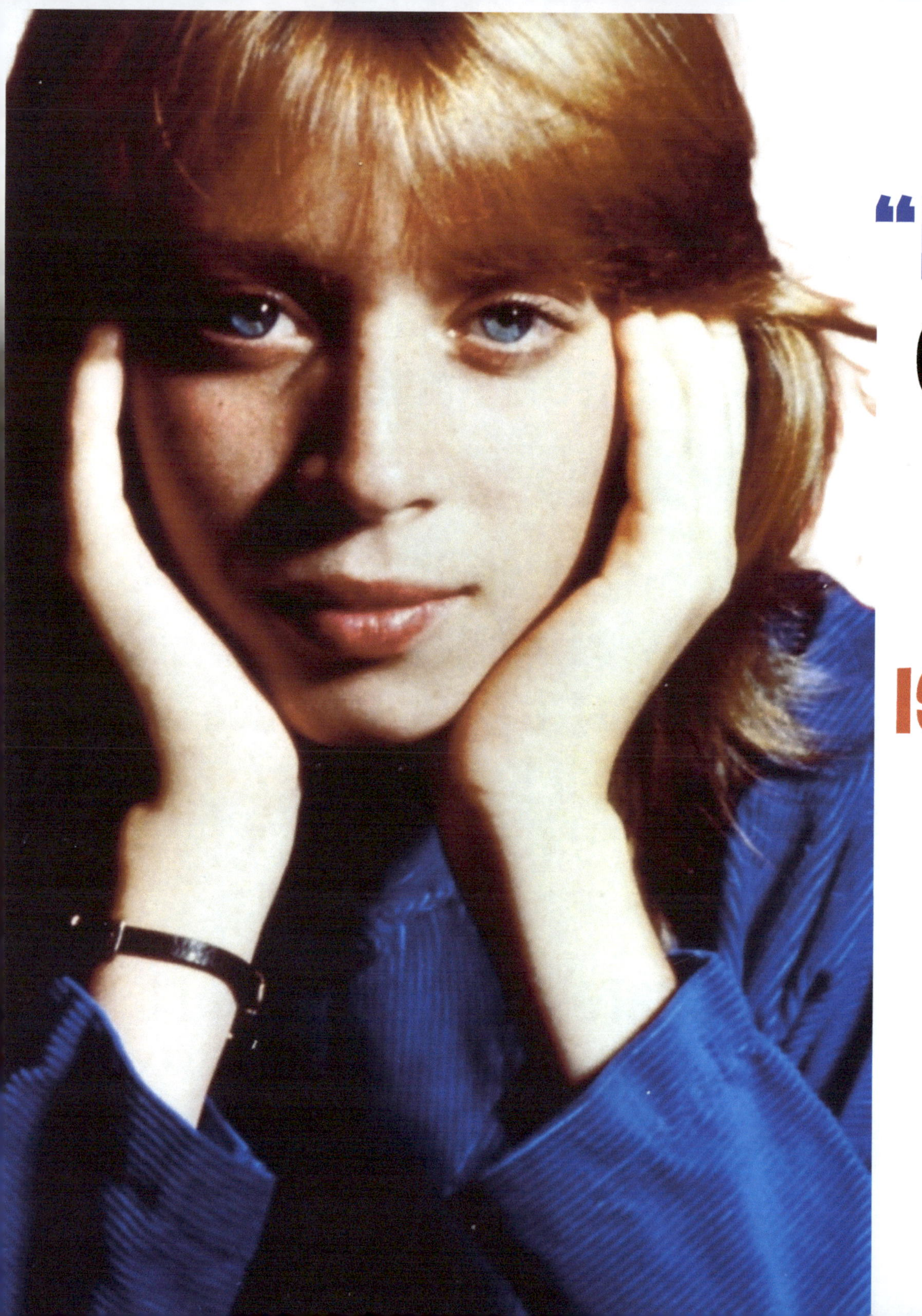

MOSES
"Let My People Go!"
God Split the Sea —
and Drowned
the Egyptians;
ISRAEL DEFENSE FORCES
Split Gaza — and
Defeated Hamas
HAPPY PASSOVER!
Sharon Esther Lampert
PRINCESS KADIMAH
8TH PROPHETESS OF ISRAEL
AM YISRAEL CHAI

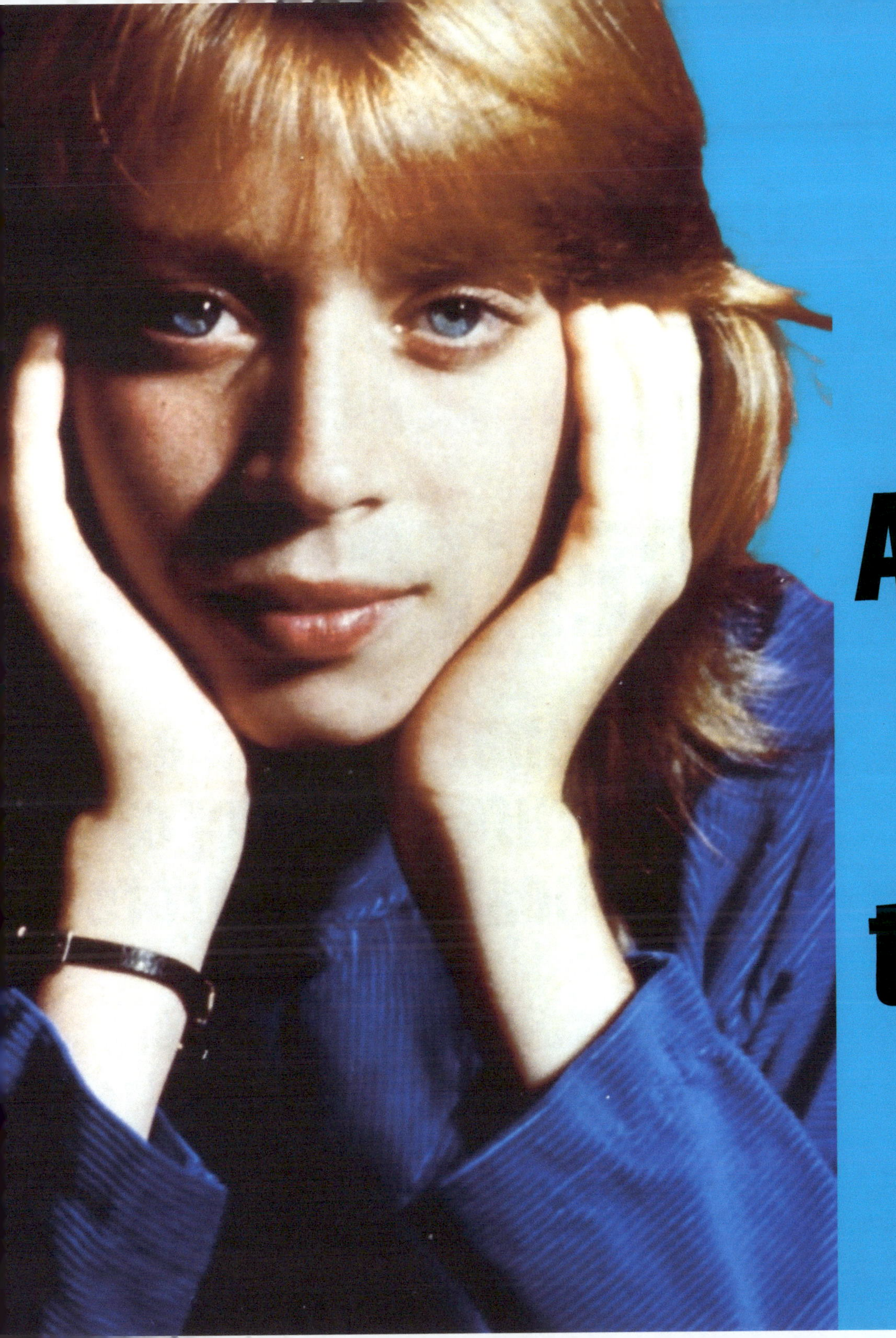

Education Cannot Amerliorate Anti-Semitism Haters Hate the Facts, the Truth, and the Light
Sharon Esther Lampert

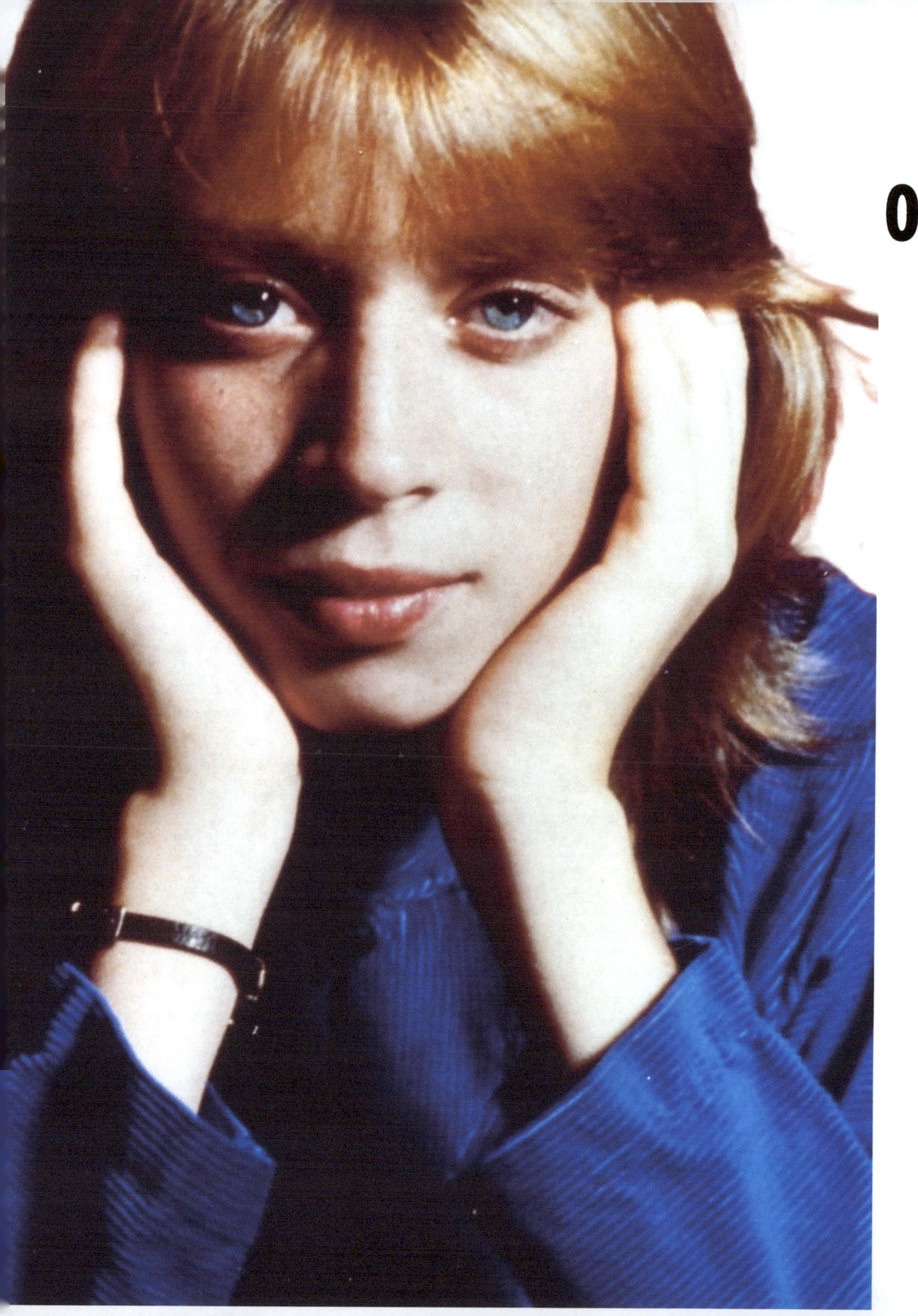

On Oct 7, 2023 —
On Simchat Torah, 6:30 A.M. —
We Read the Bible:
TOHU VAVOHU
GENESIS 1.2
Planet Earth Is a
Torture Chamber of
Unspeakable Horrors
Sharon Esther Lampert
PRINCESS KADIMAH
8TH PROPHETESS OF ISRAEL
AM YISRAEL CHAI

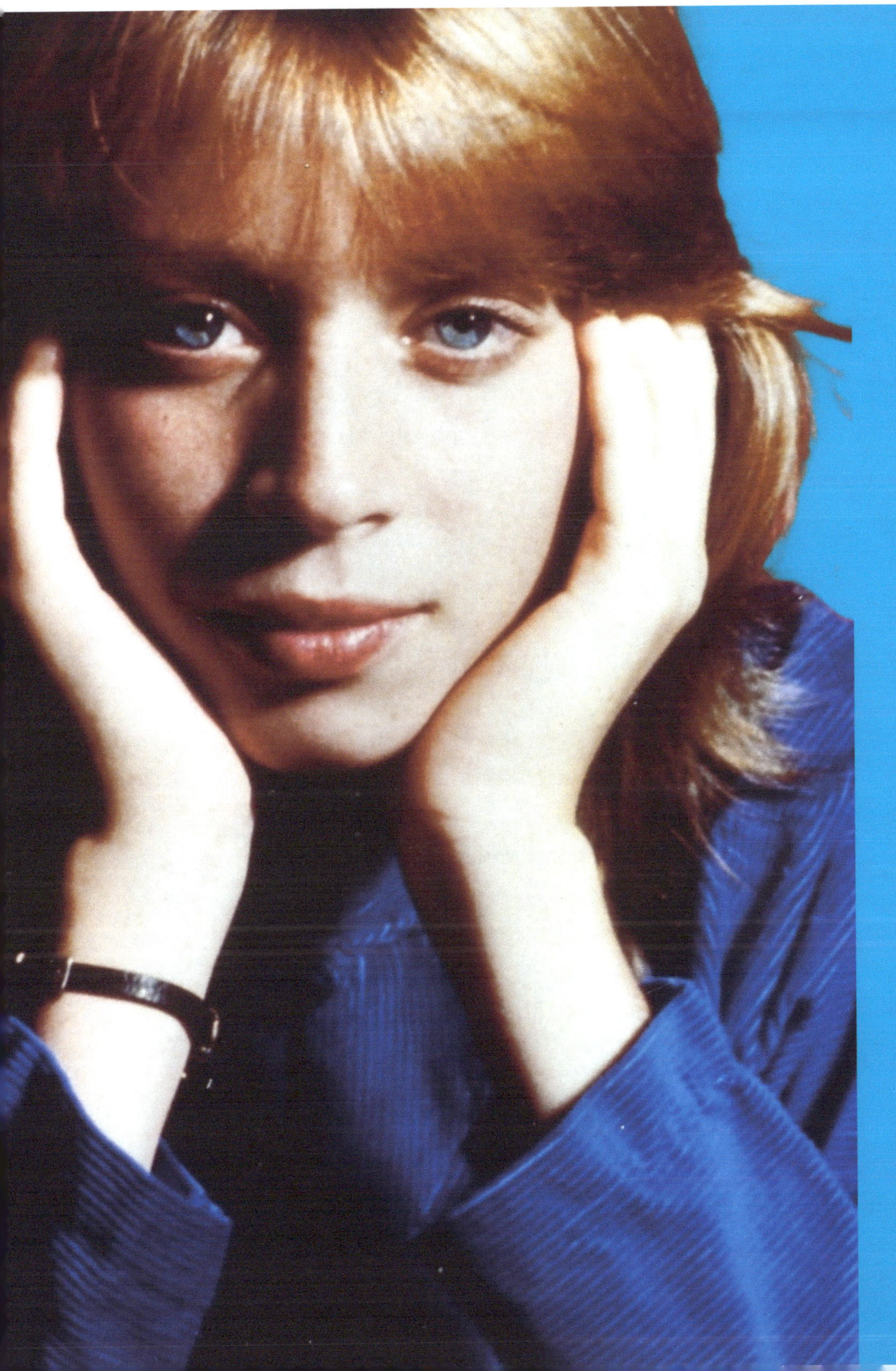

You Cannot Negotiate with Evil. Destroy the Evil or be Destroyed by the Evil.
Sharon Esther Lampert

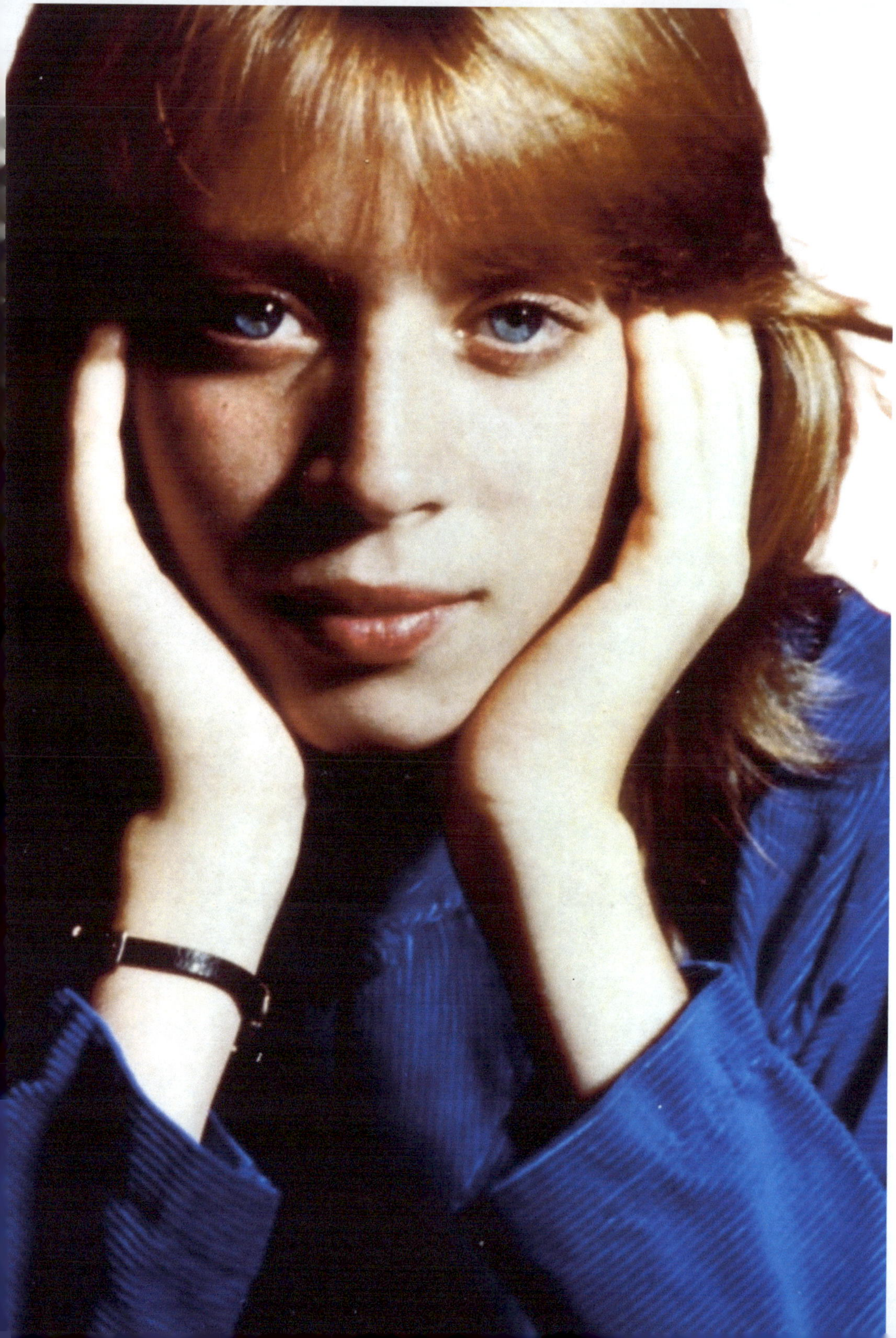

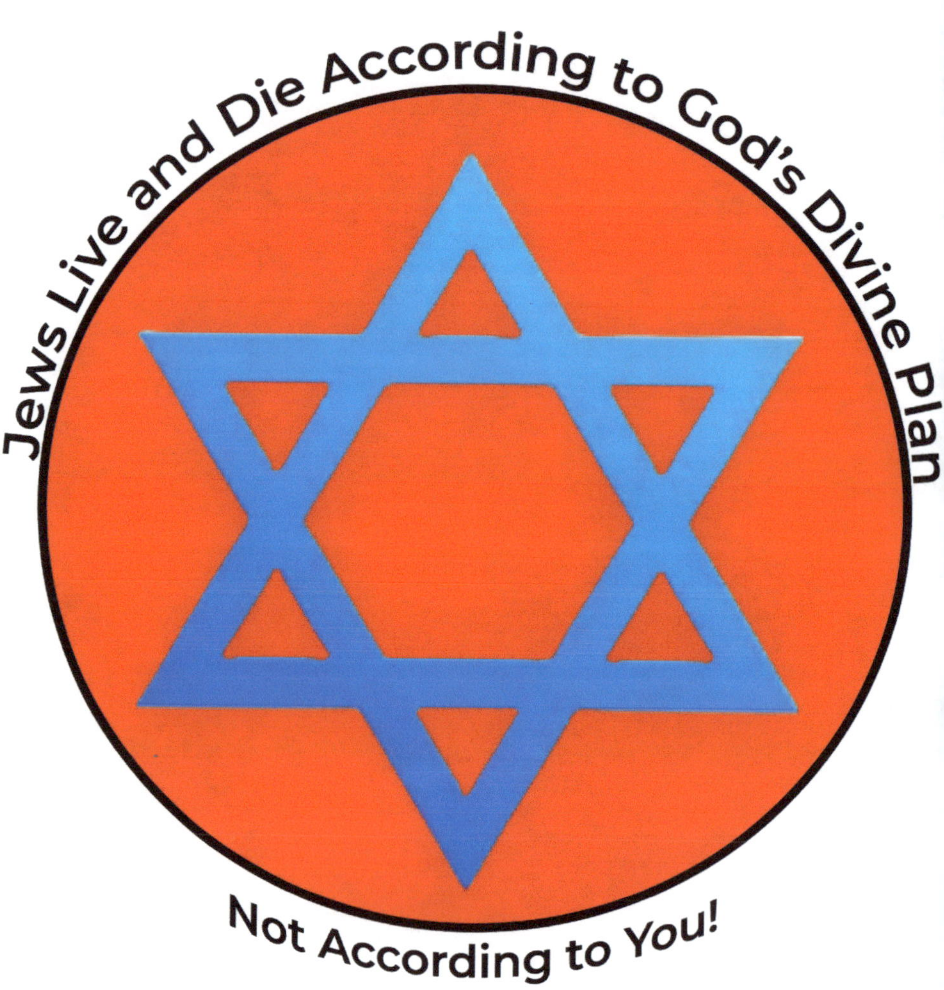

Sharon Esther Lampert
PRINCESS KADIMAH
8TH PROPHETESS OF ISRAEL
AM YISRAEL CHAI

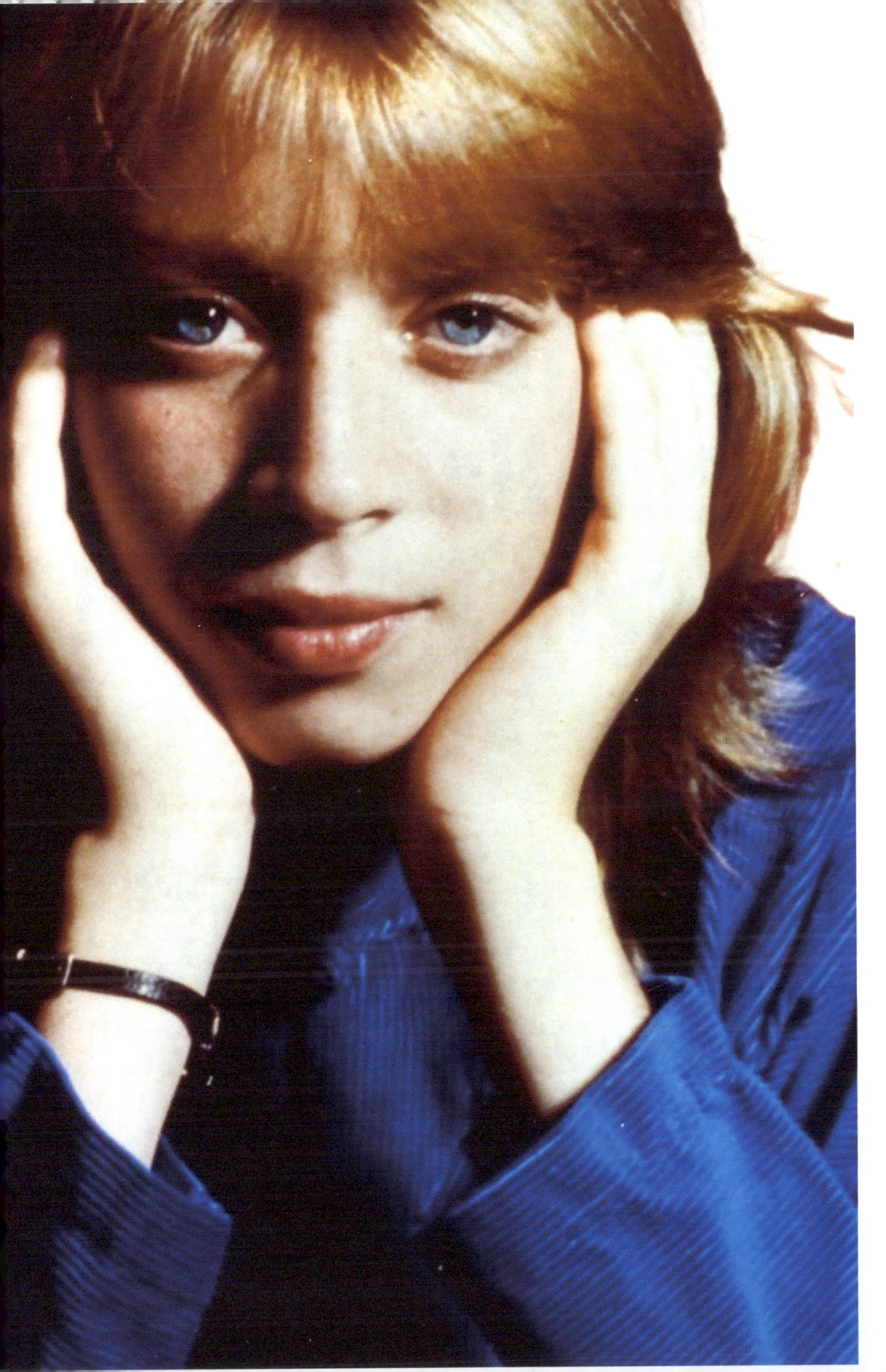

"Jews Are the
HAPPIEST
People on Planet Earth

Anti-Semites Are the
UNHAPPIEST
People on Planet Earth"

Sharon Esther Lampert
PRINCESS KADIMAH
8TH PROPHETESS OF ISRAEL
AM YISRAEL CHAI

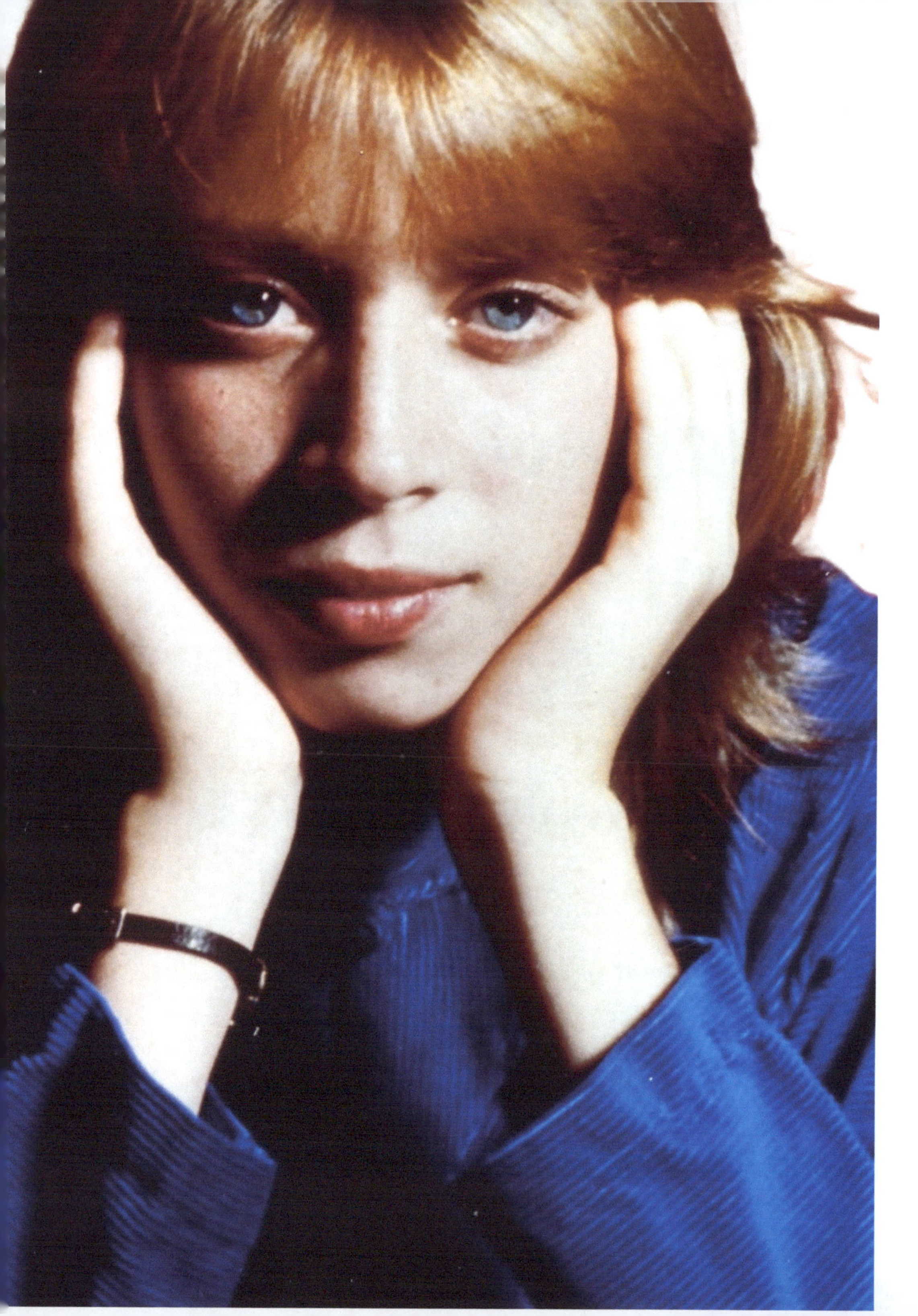

Israel Has All The Right FRIENDS, and Has All The Right ENEMIES!

Sharon Esther Lampert

PRINCESS KADIMAH

8TH PROPHETESS OF ISRAEL

AM YISRAEL CHAI

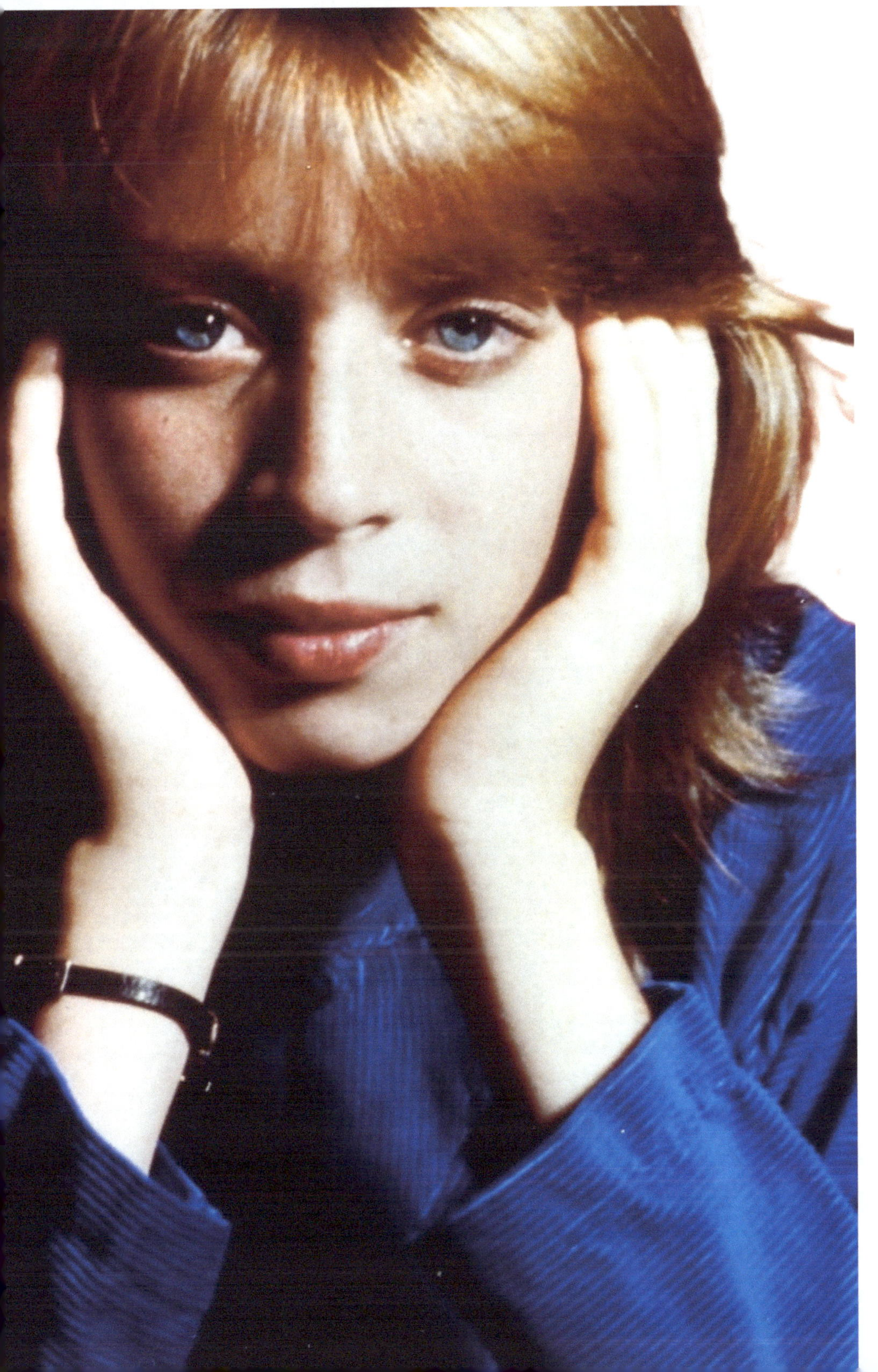

The Only **FREE ARABS** in the Middle East Live in the **DEMOCRATIC STATE of ISRAEL**

- **Religious Freedom**
- **Women's Rights**
- **LGBTQ Rights**

Sharon Esther Lampert
PRINCESS KADIMAH
8TH PROPHETESS OF ISRAEL
AM YISRAEL CHAI

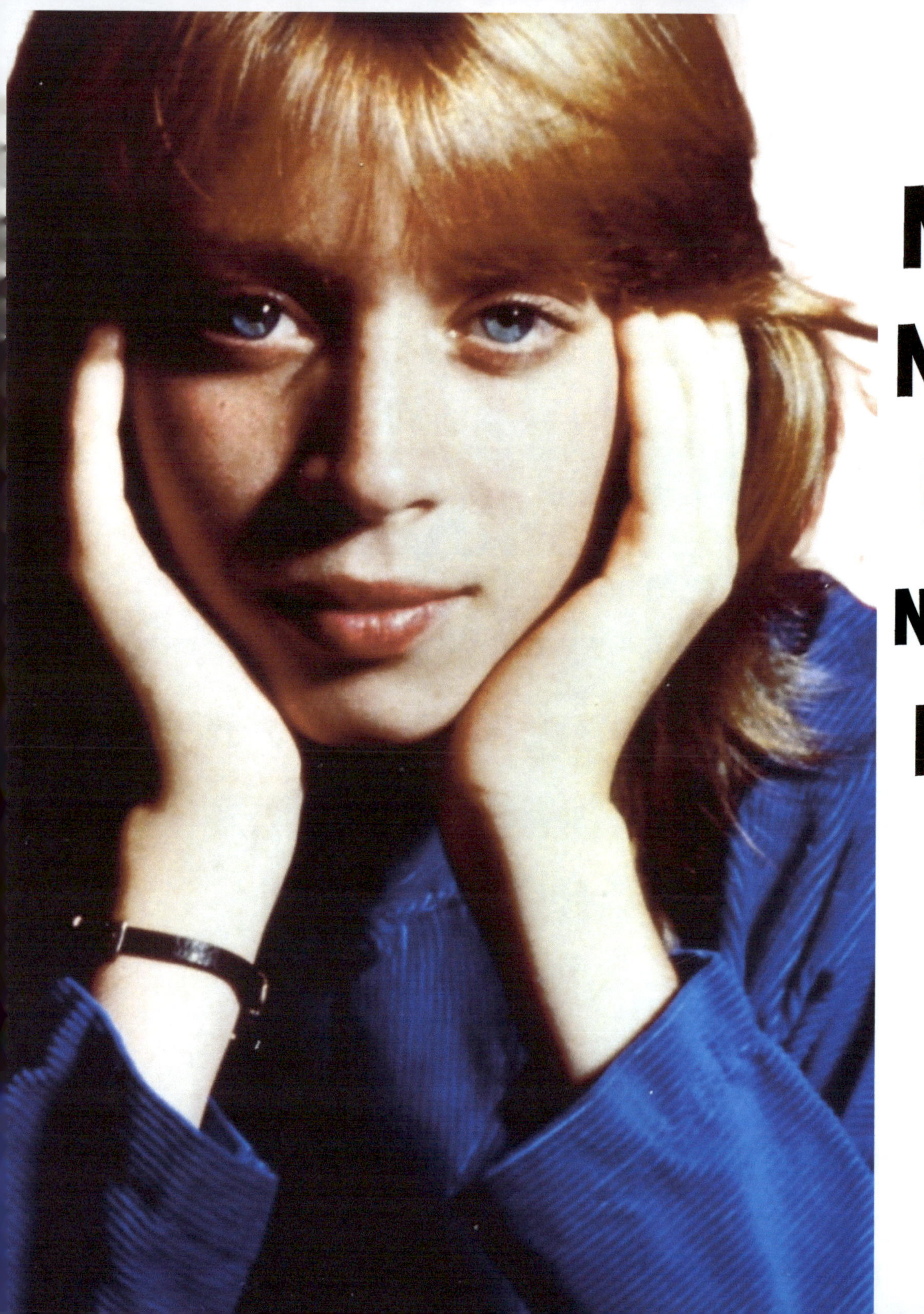

NEVER AGAIN! 1945
NEVER AGAIN IS NOW!
OCT 7, 2023
Never Forgive! Never Forget!
NOW OR NEVER! IRAN
Sharon Esther Lampert
PRINCESS KADIMAH
8TH PROPHETESS OF ISRAEL
AM YISRAEL CHAI

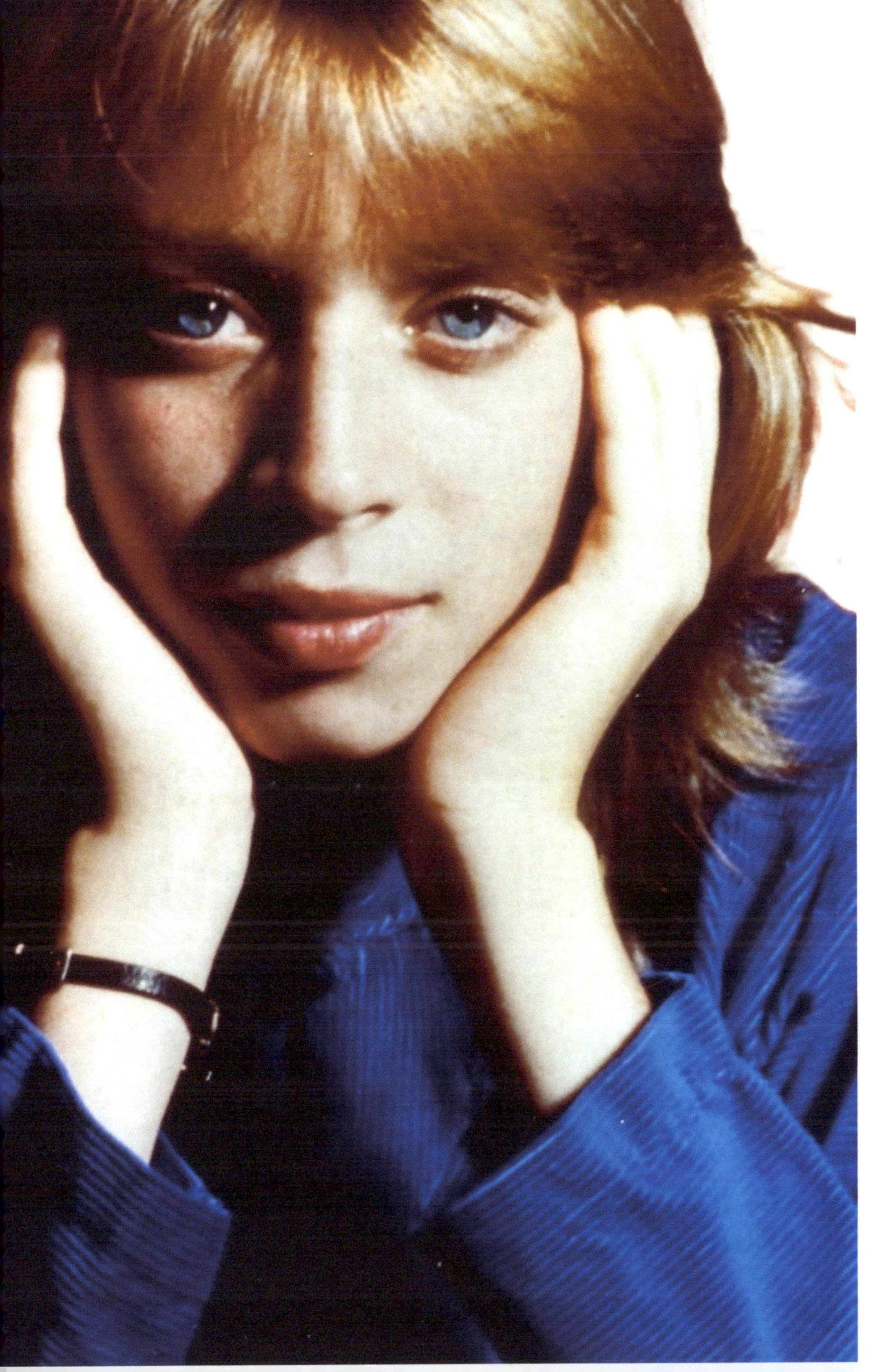

For 18 Years, ISRAEL Supplies GAZA with Water, Food, Fuel, Electricity, and Jobs.

For 18 Years, IRAN Supplies GAZA with Arms to Destroy Israel

Sharon Esther Lampert
PRINCESS KADIMAH
8TH PROPHETESS OF ISRAEL
AM YISRAEL CHAI

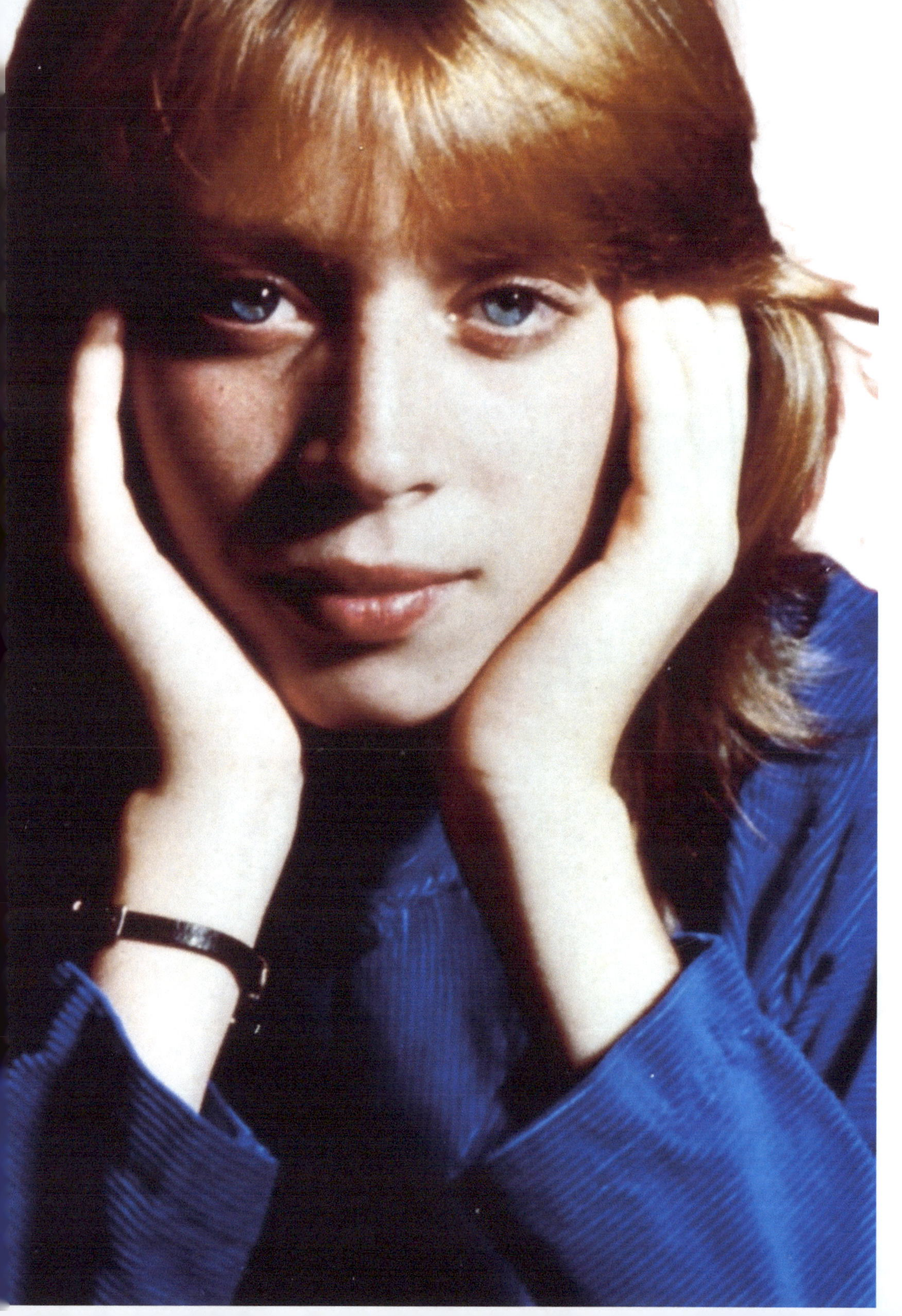

"On April 13, 2024
Iran's 300+ killing
machines could
have destroyed
Islam's 3rd holiest
Al Aqsa Mosque.
God speaks in whispers,
and helicopter crashes!"

Sharon Esther Lampert
PRINCESS KADIMAH
8TH PROPHETESS OF ISRAEL
AM YISRAEL CHAI

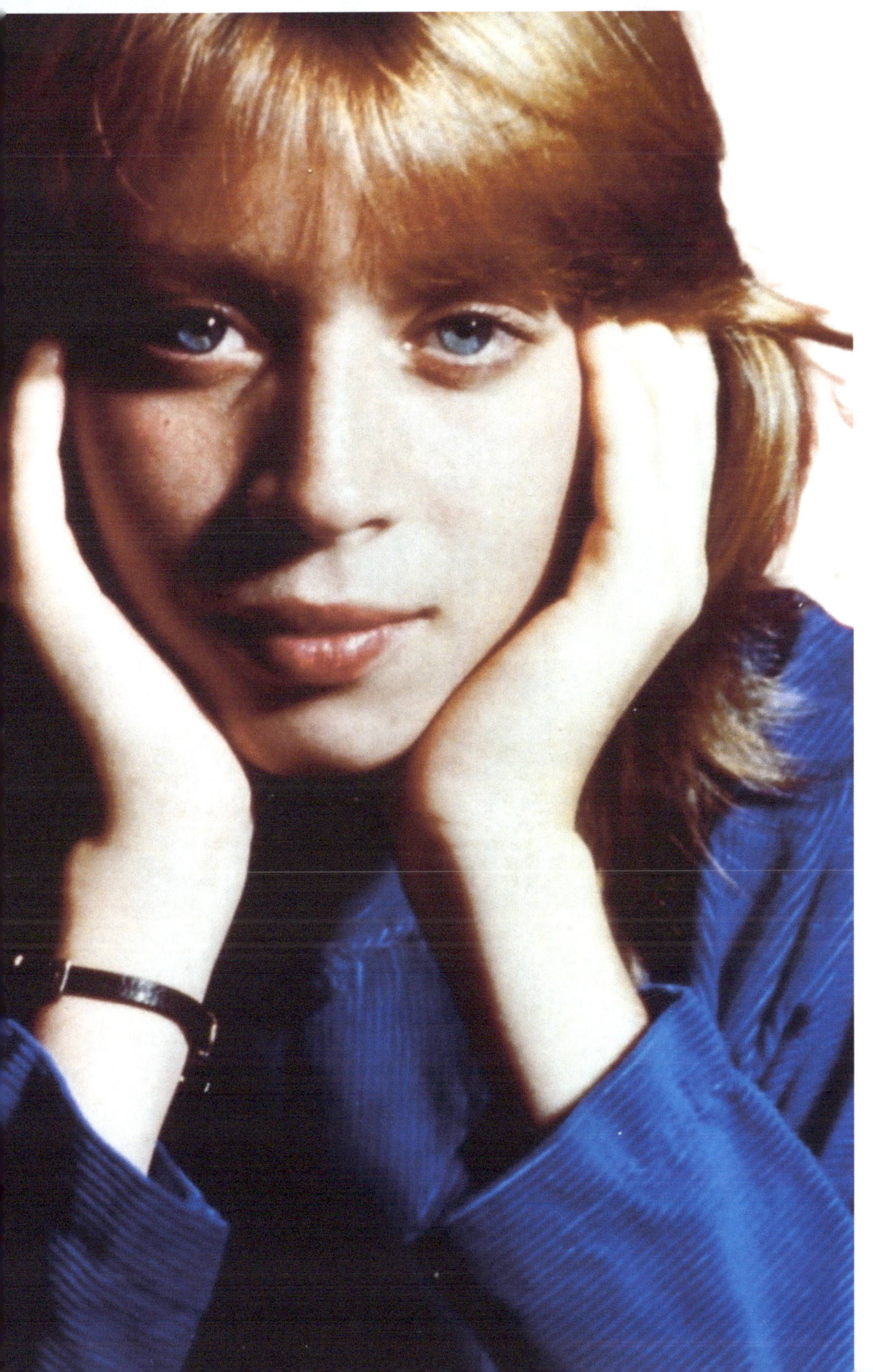

HAMAS Took The Whole World Hostage!

Jews
Christians
Muslims
Hindus
Buddhists

Sharon Esther Lampert
PRINCESS KADIMAH
8TH PROPHETESS OF ISRAEL
AM YISRAEL CHAI

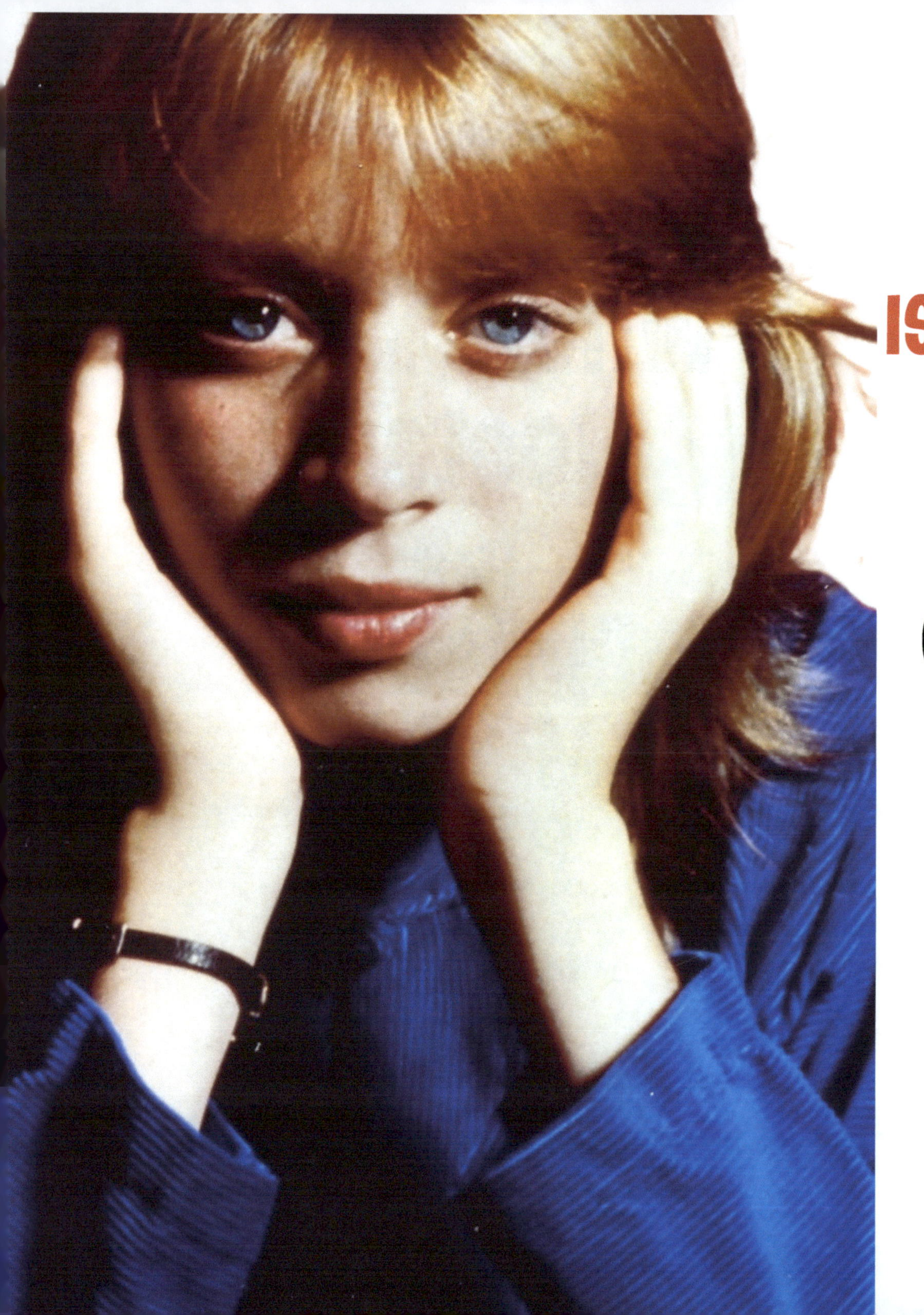

Entire Countries Are Hijacked By
ISLAMIC JIHAD TERRORISTS

Lebanon: Hezbollah
Yemen: Houthis
Gaza: Hamas, PIJ, ++++
Syria: ISIS, Al-Qaeda
Afghanistan: Taliban
Iran: Ayatollah

Sharon Esther Lampert
PRINCESS KADIMAH
8TH PROPHETESS OF ISRAEL
AM YISRAEL CHAI

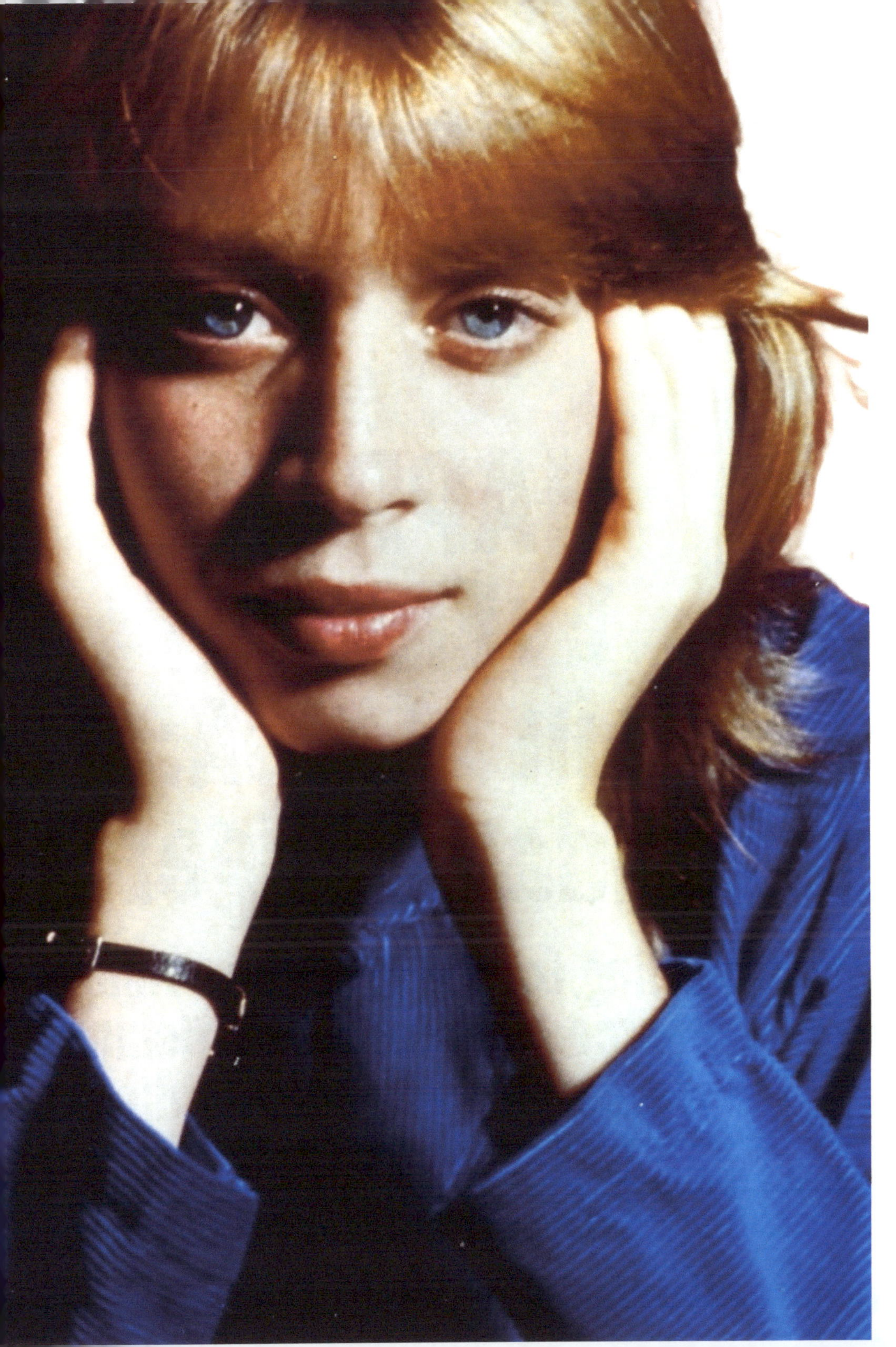

For 36 Years HAMAS Murdered Innocent Civilians of All Nationalities

Ticking-Time Bomb!

Sharon Esther Lampert
PRINCESS KADIMAH
8TH PROPHETESS OF ISRAEL
AM YISRAEL CHAI

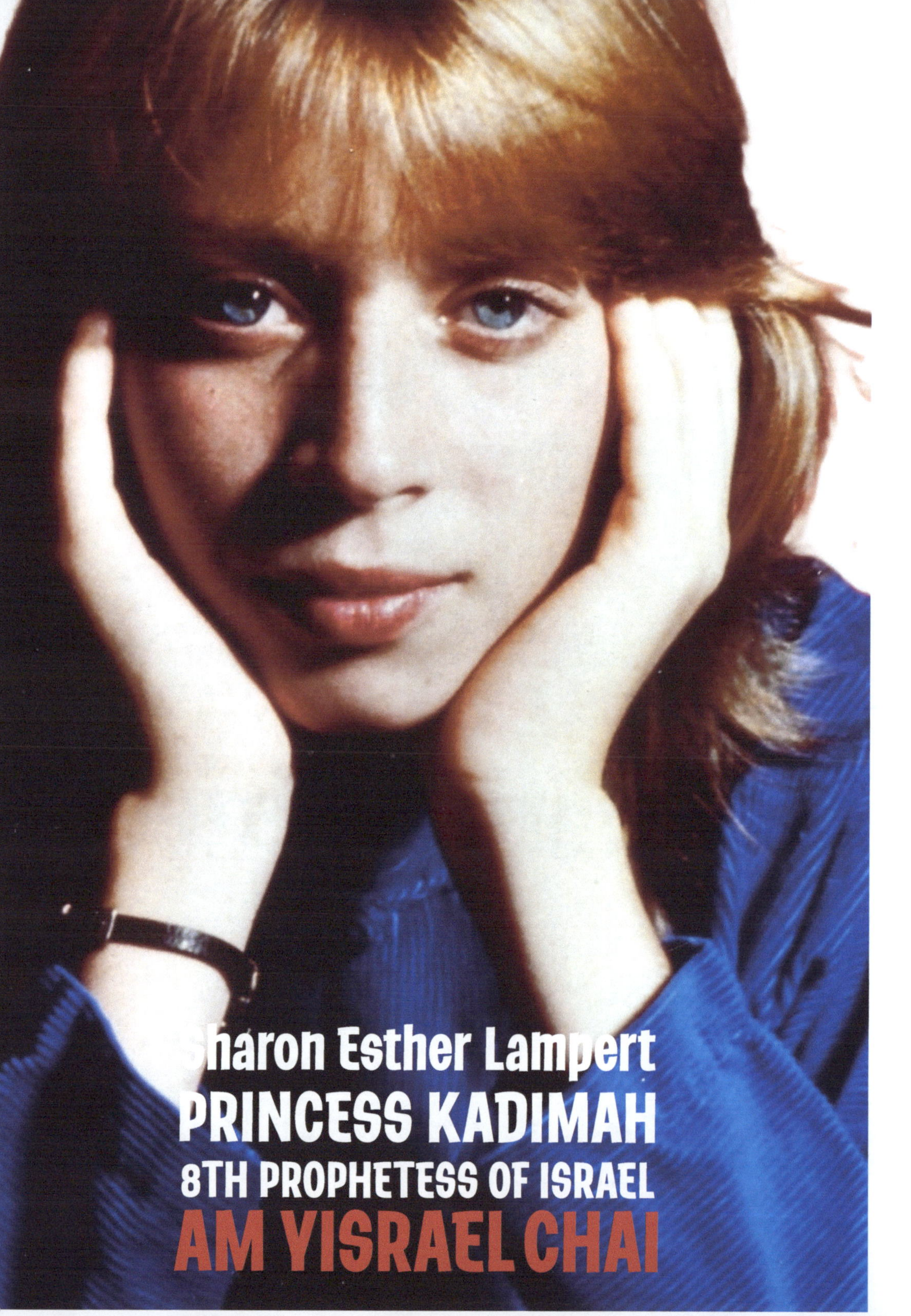

FOR CENTURIES
OCT 7
HAPPENS EVERY DAY in AFRICA: Sudan & Nigeria

Raiding, Looting & Burning Villages
Forced Conversions to Islam
Forced Marriages to Soldiers
Forced Sexual Assaults
Forced Child Soldiers
Forced Martrys for Islamic Jihad

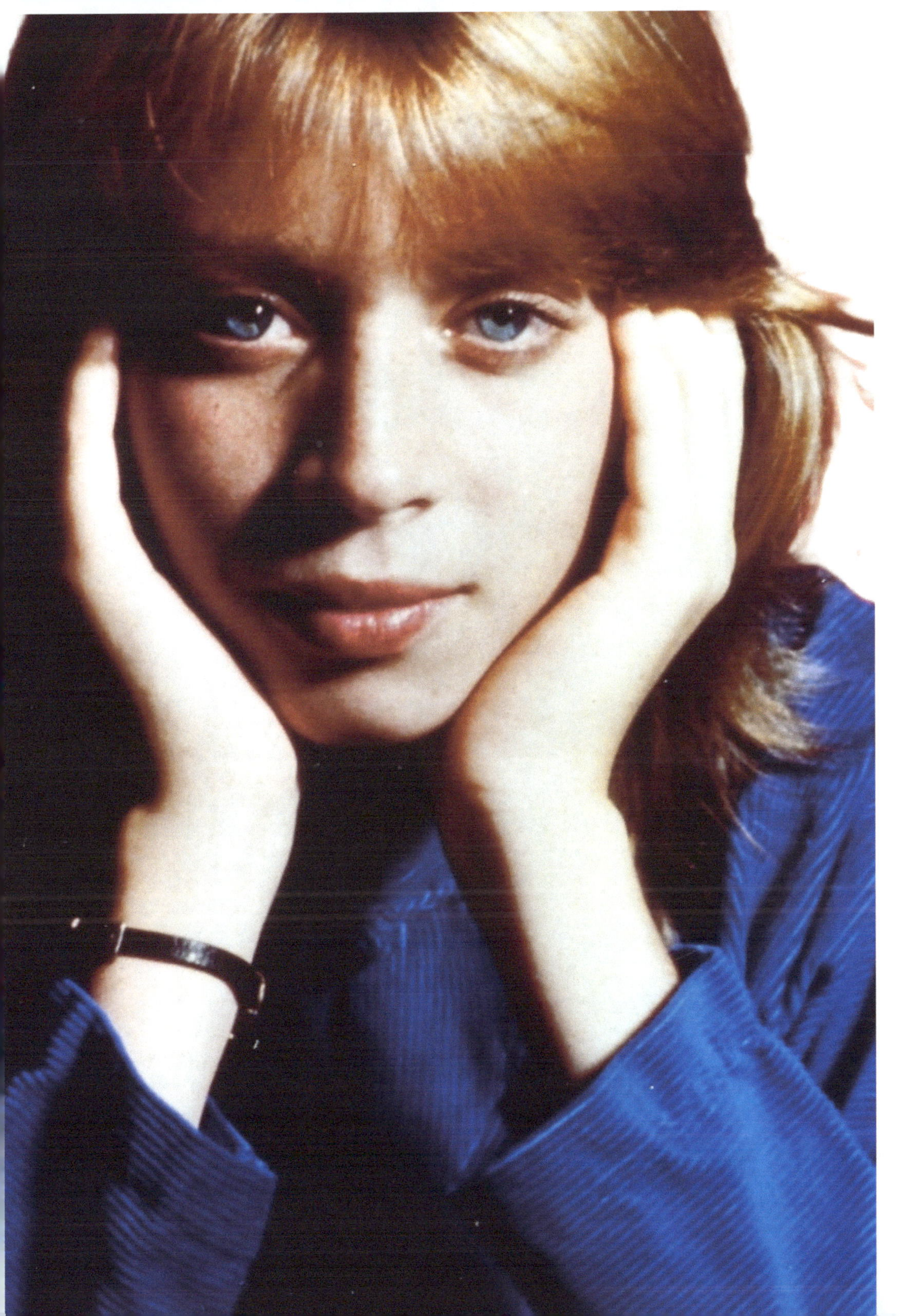

BROKEN WORLD OF BROKEN PEOPLE

Sharon Esther Lampert
PRINCESS KADIMAH
8TH PROPHETESS OF ISRAEL
AM YISRAEL CHAI

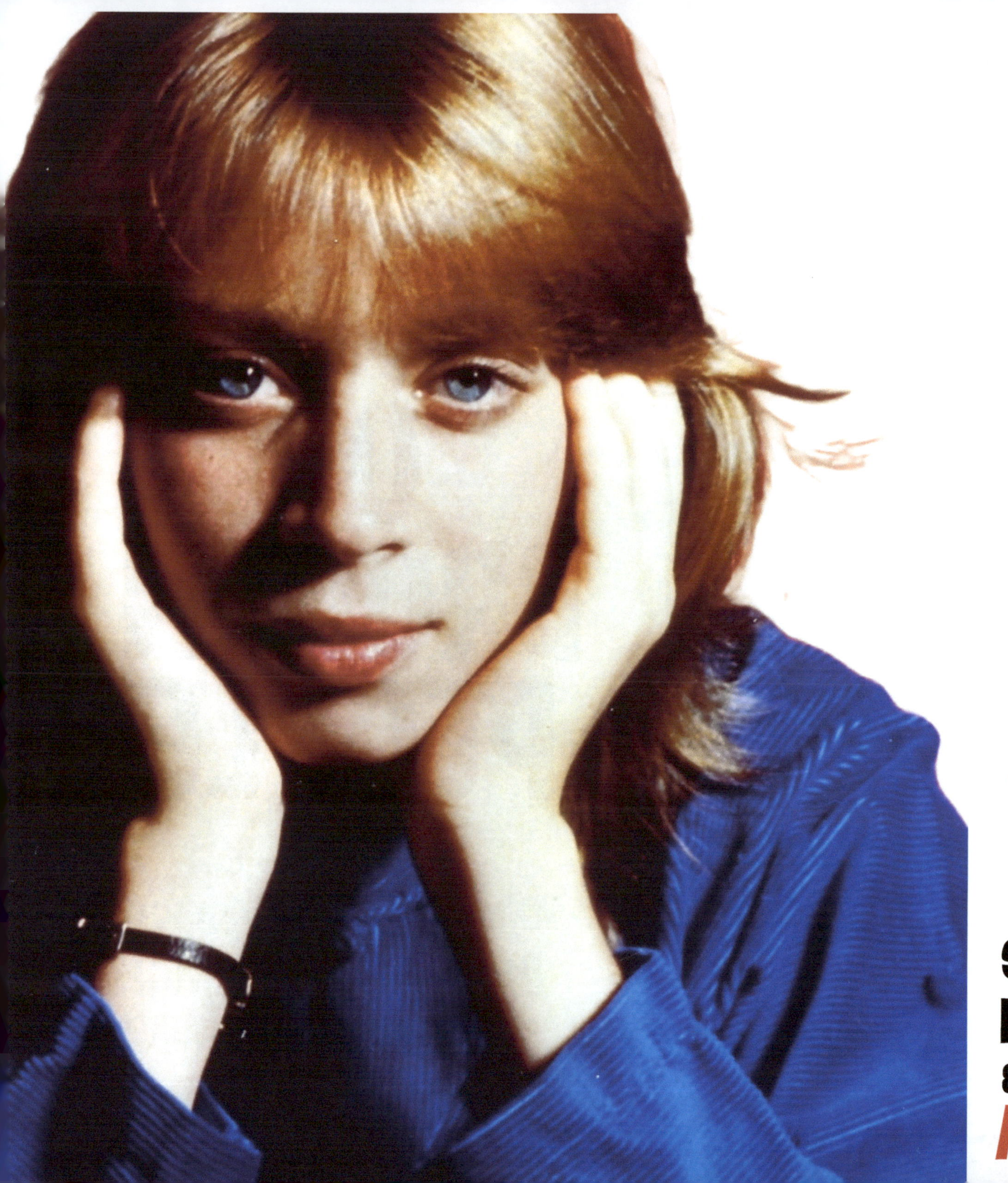

HAMAS
IS A
FOOD
TRUCK
AWAY
FROM
DEFEAT

Sharon Esther Lampert
PRINCESS KADIMAH
8TH PROPHETESS OF ISRAEL
AM YISRAEL CHAI

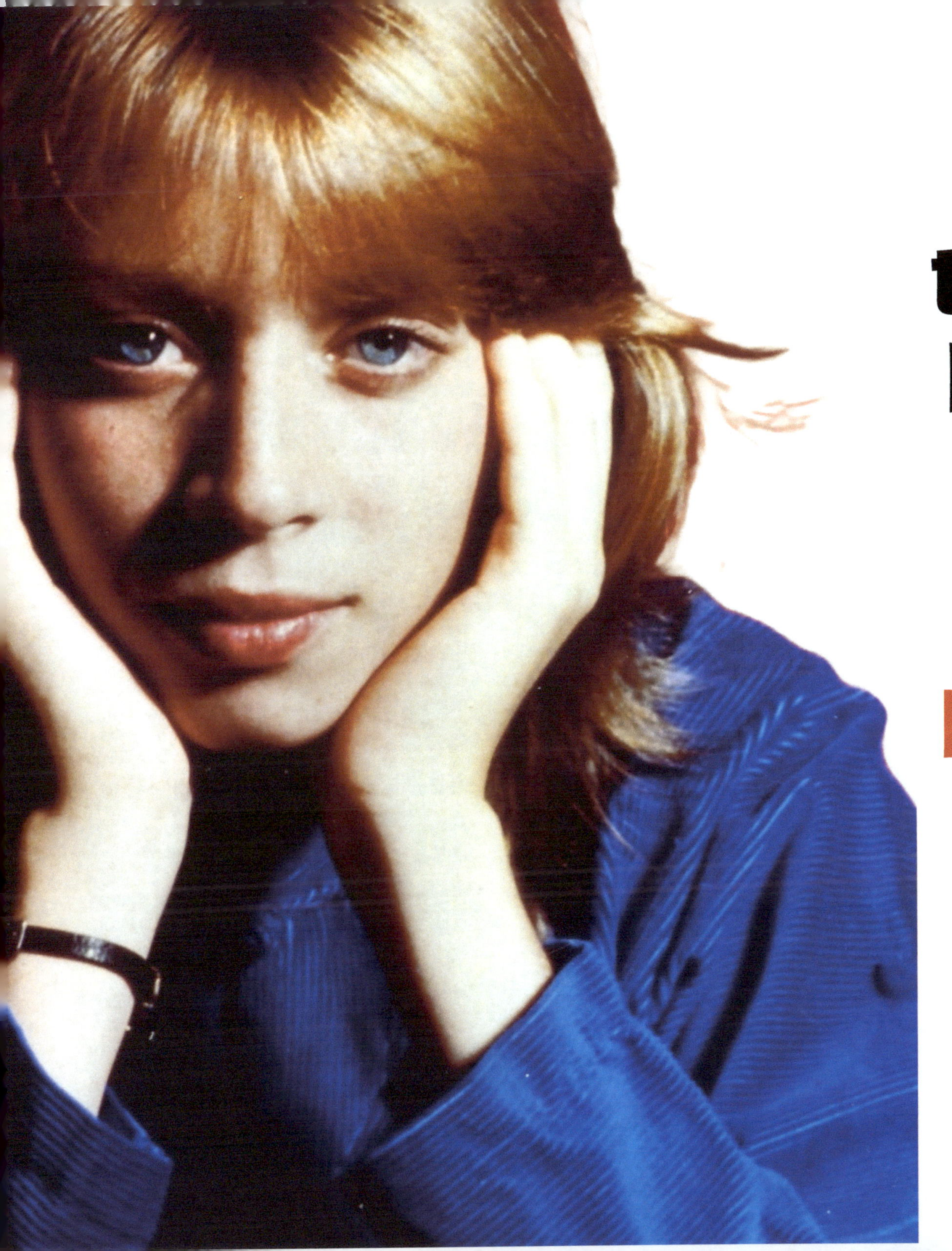

Terrorists Always Have the Advantage Because They Play by Their Own Rules!

PLAY THEM OR GET PLAYED BY THEM!

THE SYSTEM WILL FAIL BEFORE IT SUCCEEDS

Sharon Esther Lampert
PRINCESS KADIMAH
8TH PROPHETESS OF ISRAEL
AM YISRAEL CHAI

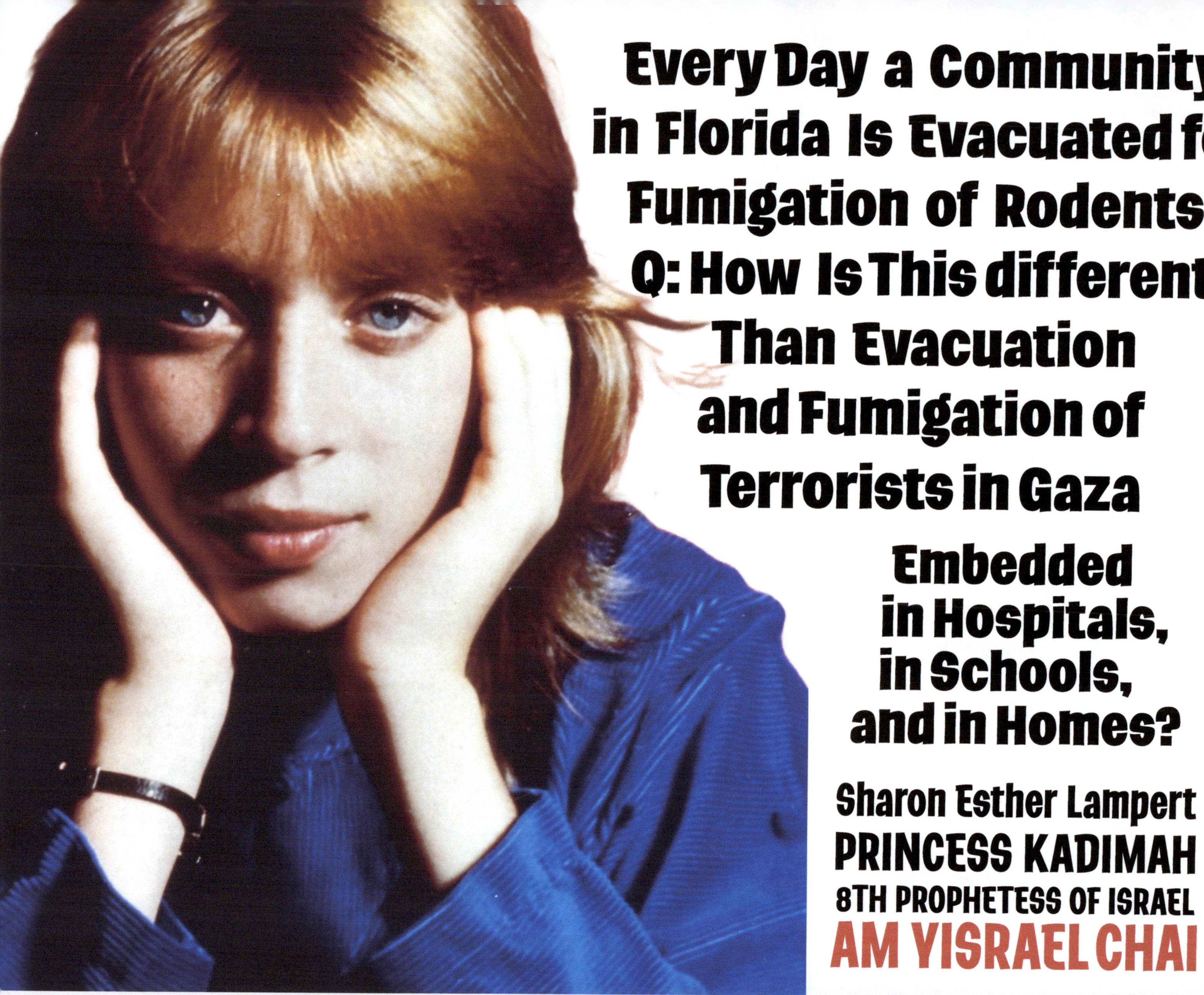

Every Day a Community in Florida Is Evacuated for Fumigation of Rodents.
Q: How Is This different Than Evacuation and Fumigation of Terrorists in Gaza
Embedded in Hospitals, in Schools, and in Homes?
Sharon Esther Lampert
PRINCESS KADIMAH
8TH PROPHETESS OF ISRAEL
AM YISRAEL CHAI

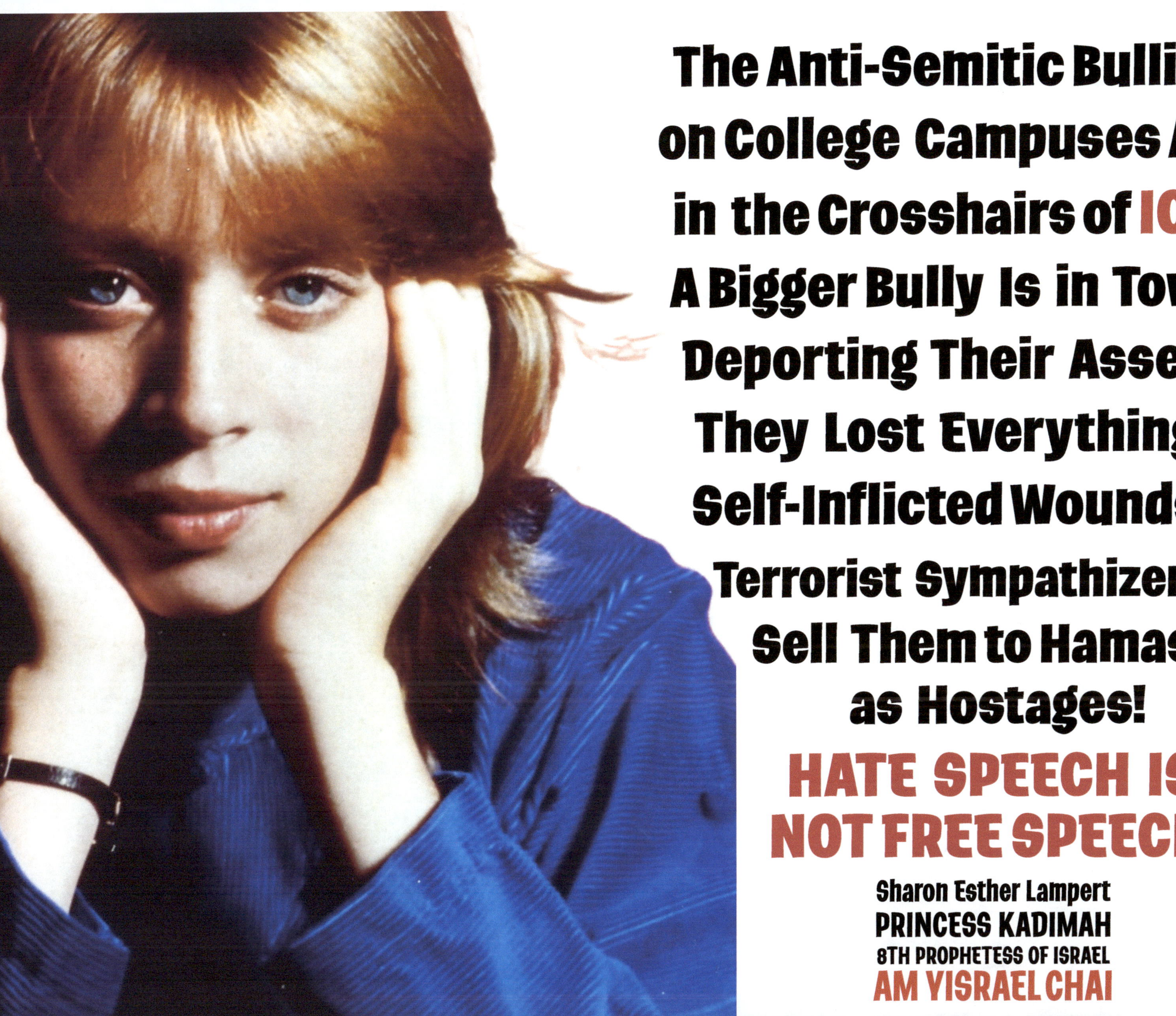

The Anti-Semitic Bullies on College Campuses Are in the Crosshairs of ICE. A Bigger Bully Is in Town Deporting Their Asses. They Lost Everything! Self-Inflicted Wounds!
Terrorist Sympathizers! Sell Them to Hamas as Hostages!
HATE SPEECH IS NOT FREE SPEECH!
Sharon Esther Lampert
PRINCESS KADIMAH
8TH PROPHETESS OF ISRAEL
AM YISRAEL CHAI

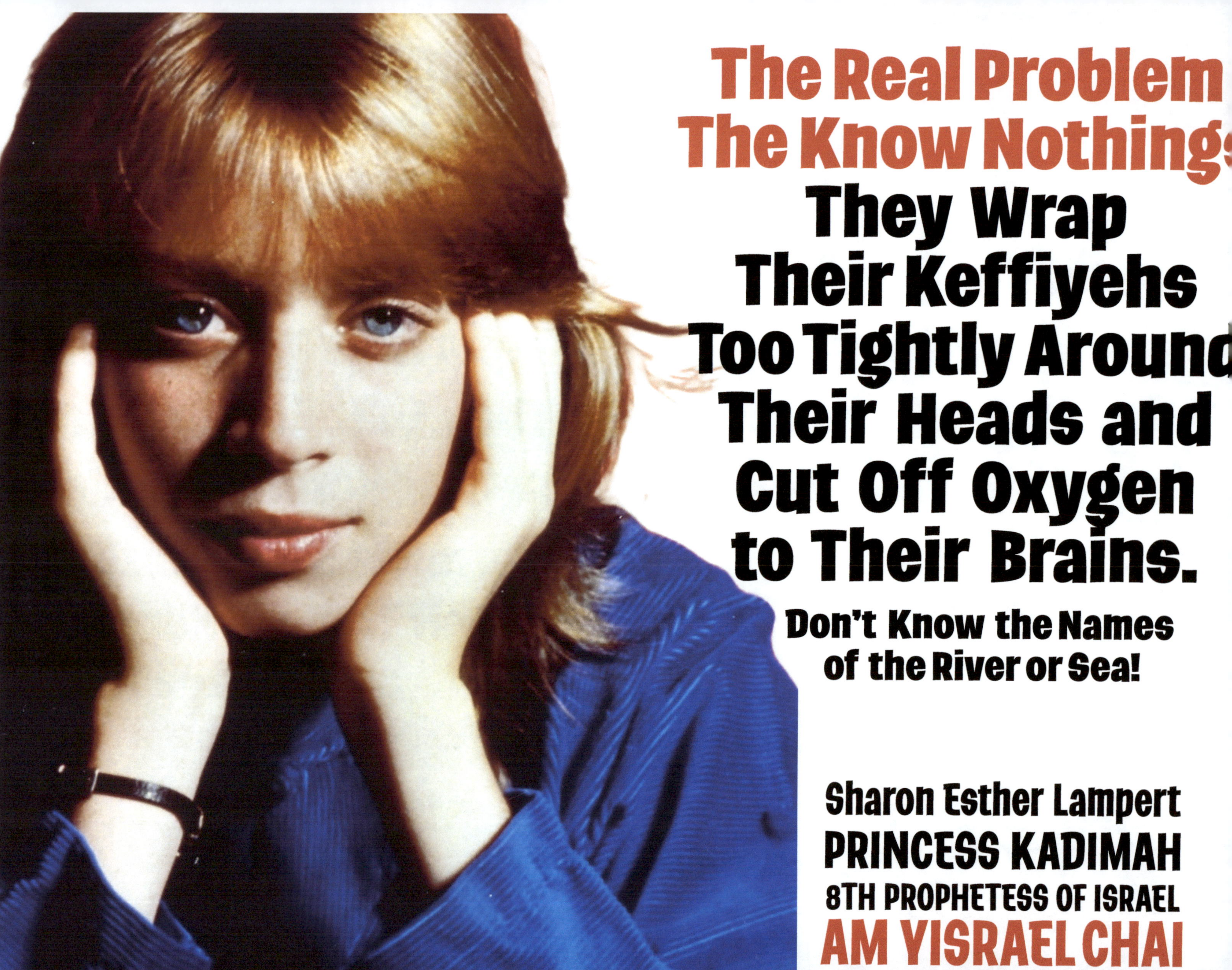
The Real Problem
The Know Nothings
They Wrap
Their Keffiyehs
Too Tightly Around
Their Heads and
Cut Off Oxygen
to Their Brains.
Don't Know the Names
of the River or Sea!
Sharon Esther Lampert
PRINCESS KADIMAH
8TH PROPHETESS OF ISRAEL
AM YISRAEL CHAI

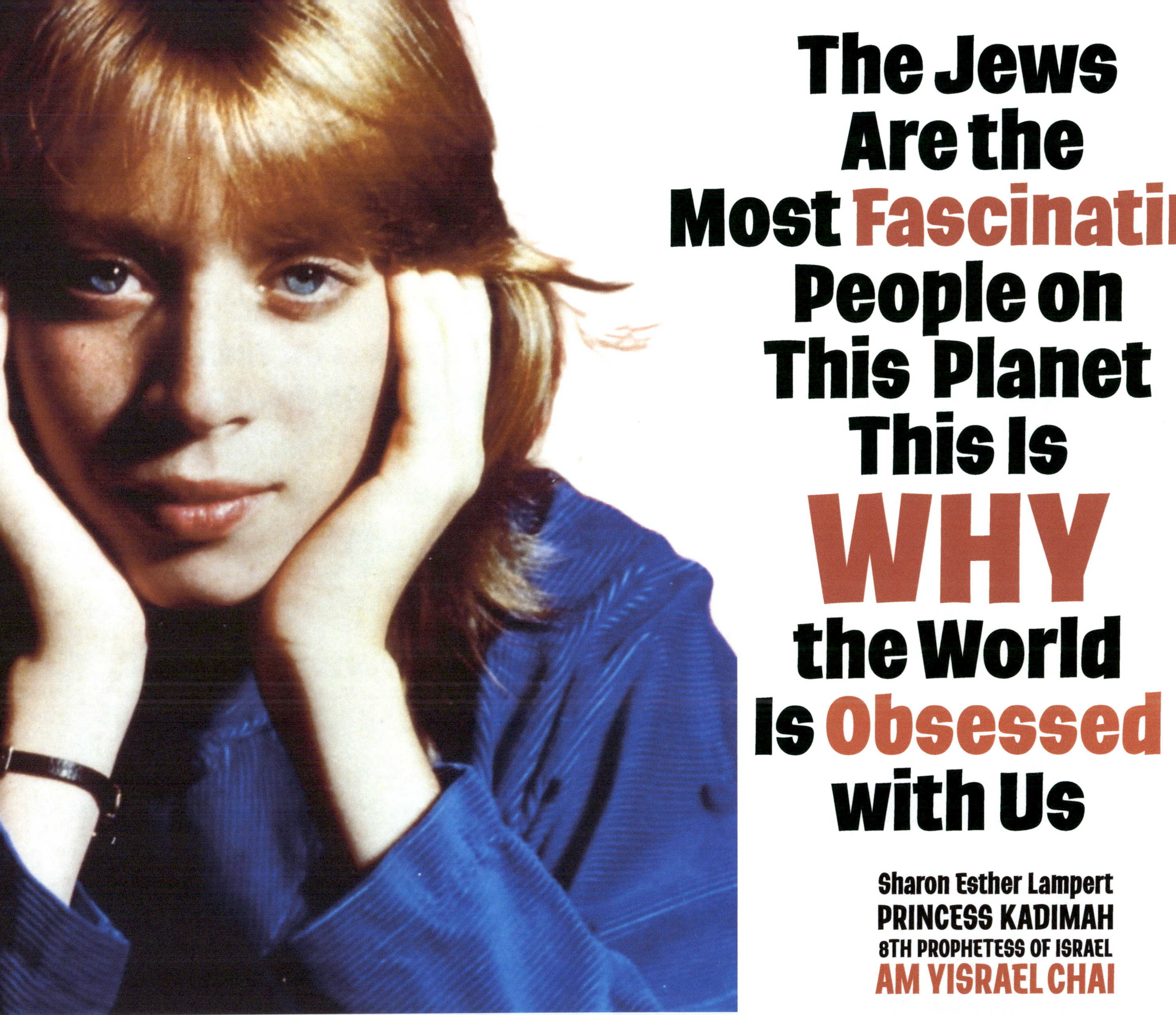

The Jews Are the Most Fascinating People on This Planet This Is WHY the World Is Obsessed with Us
Sharon Esther Lampert
PRINCESS KADIMAH
8TH PROPHETESS OF ISRAEL
AM YISRAEL CHAI

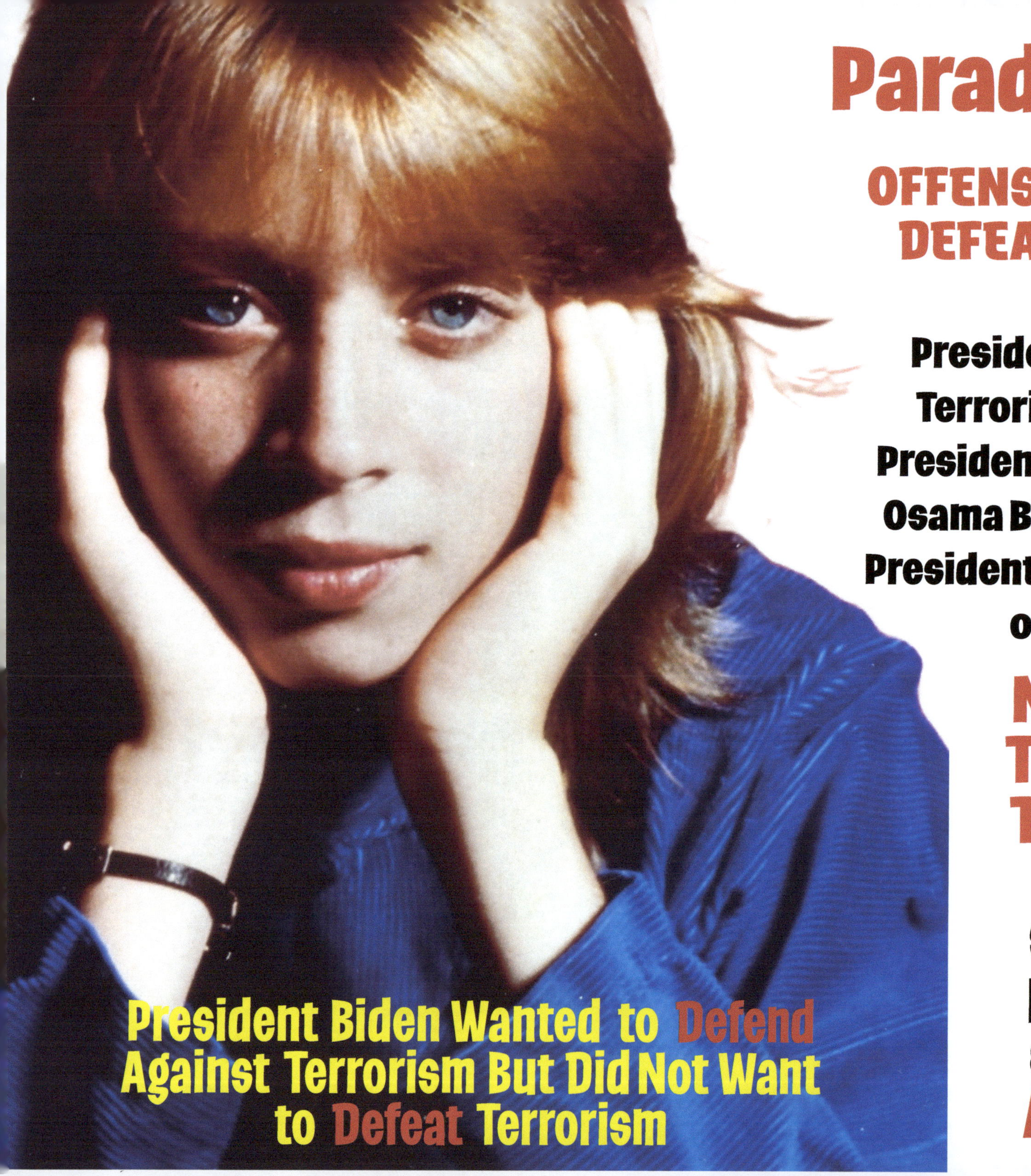
Paradigm Shift 1
OFFENSE Over DEFENSE
DEFEAT Over DEFEND
Since 911,
President Bush Defeated
Terrorists on Their Turf!
President Obama Neutralized
Osama Bin Laden on His Turf!
President Trump Defeated ISIS
on Their Turf!
NEUTRALIZE THREATS ON THEIR TURF!
Sharon Esther Lampert
PRINCESS KADIMAH
8TH PROPHETESS OF ISRAEL
AM YISRAEL CHAI
President Biden Wanted to Defend Against Terrorism But Did Not Want to Defeat Terrorism

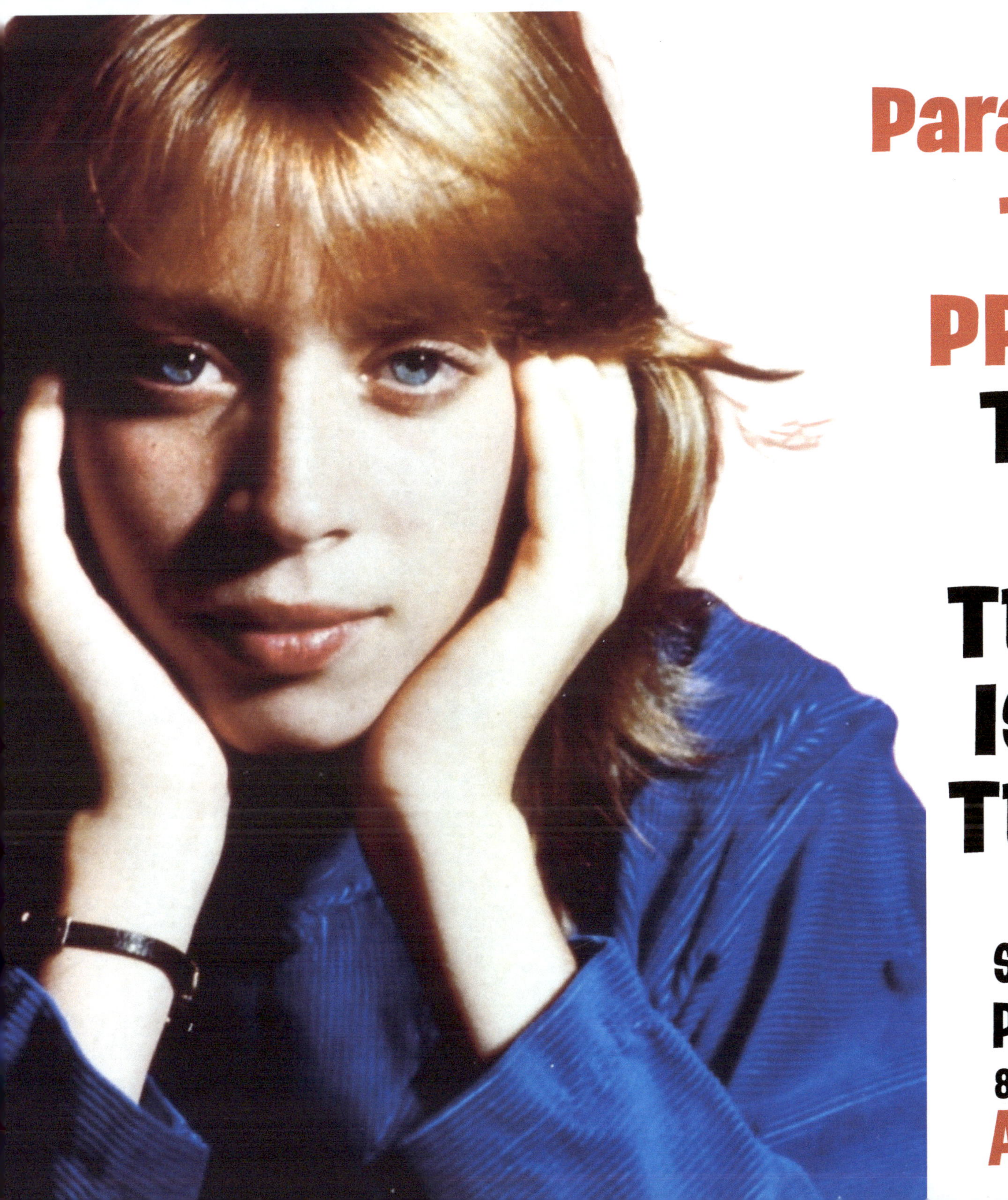

Paradigm Shift 2
TAKE NO PRISONERS!
THE ONLY GOOD TERRORIST IS A DEAD TERRORIST
Sharon Esther Lampert
PRINCESS KADIMAH
8TH PROPHETESS OF ISRAEL
AM YISRAEL CHAI

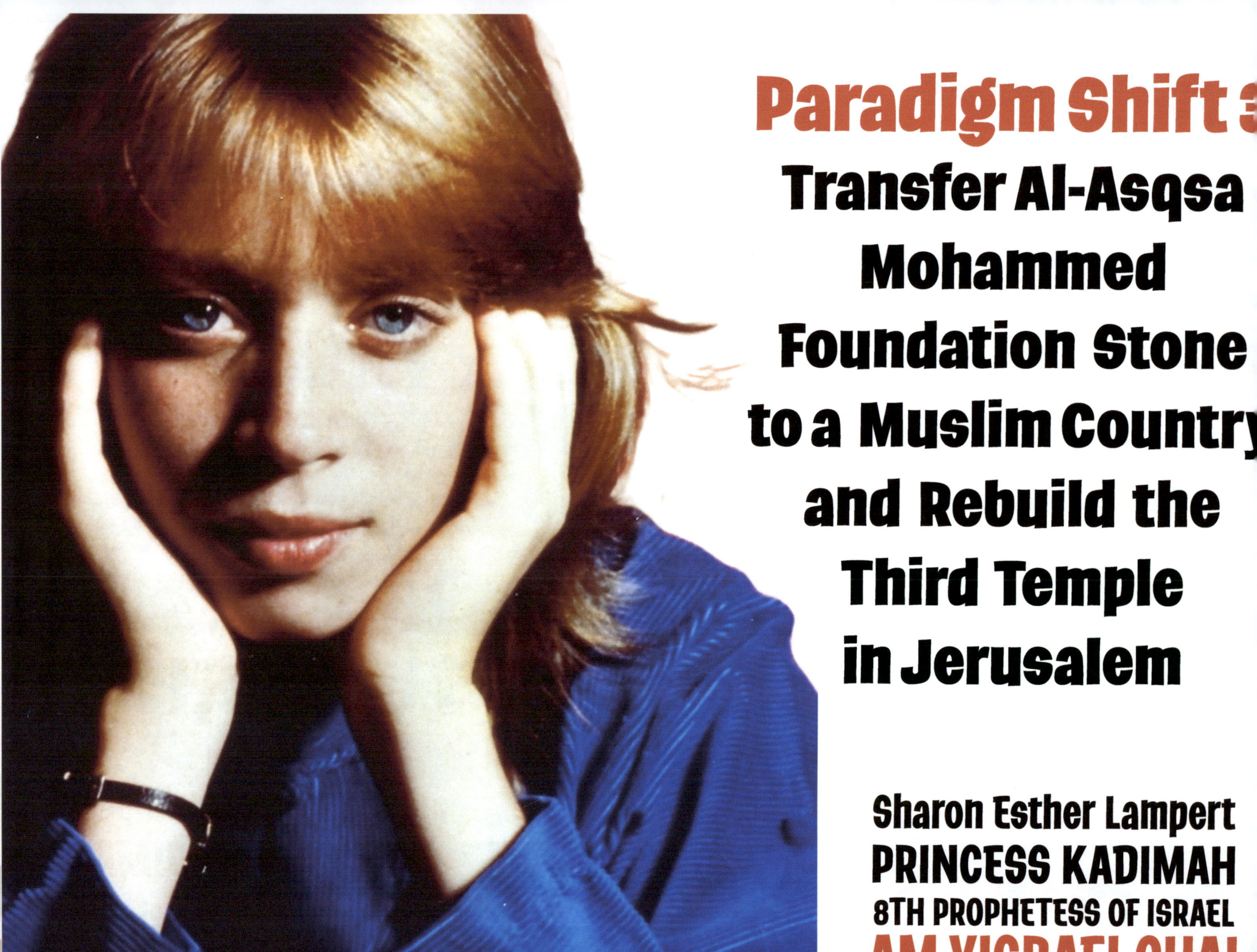
Paradigm Shift 3:
Transfer Al-Asqsa Mohammed Foundation Stone to a Muslim Country and Rebuild the Third Temple in Jerusalem

Sharon Esther Lampert
PRINCESS KADIMAH
8TH PROPHETESS OF ISRAEL
AM YISRAEL CHAI

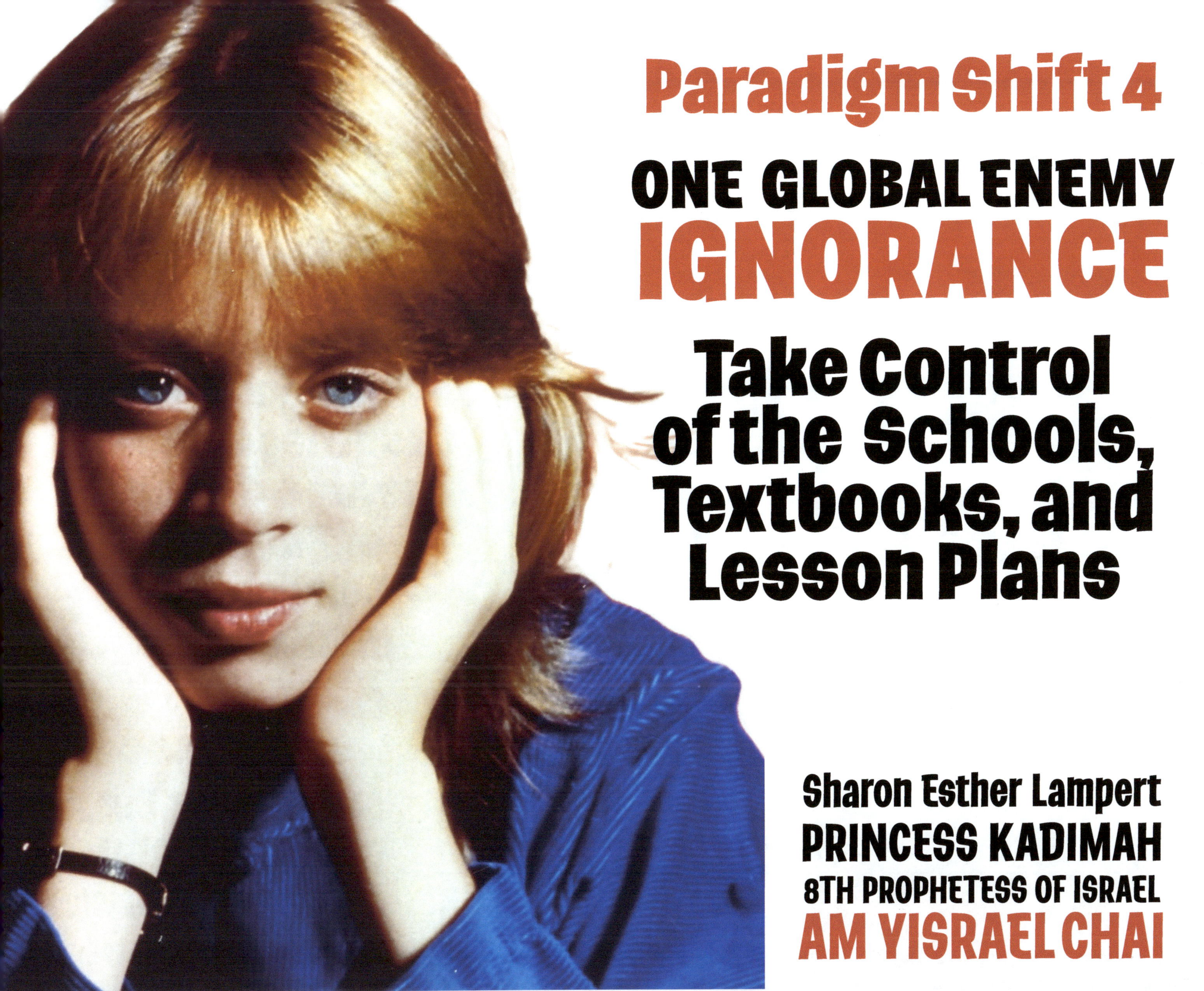

Paradigm Shift 4
ONE GLOBAL ENEMY
IGNORANCE
Take Control of the Schools, Textbooks, and Lesson Plans
Sharon Esther Lampert
PRINCESS KADIMAH
8TH PROPHETESS OF ISRAEL
AM YISRAEL CHAI

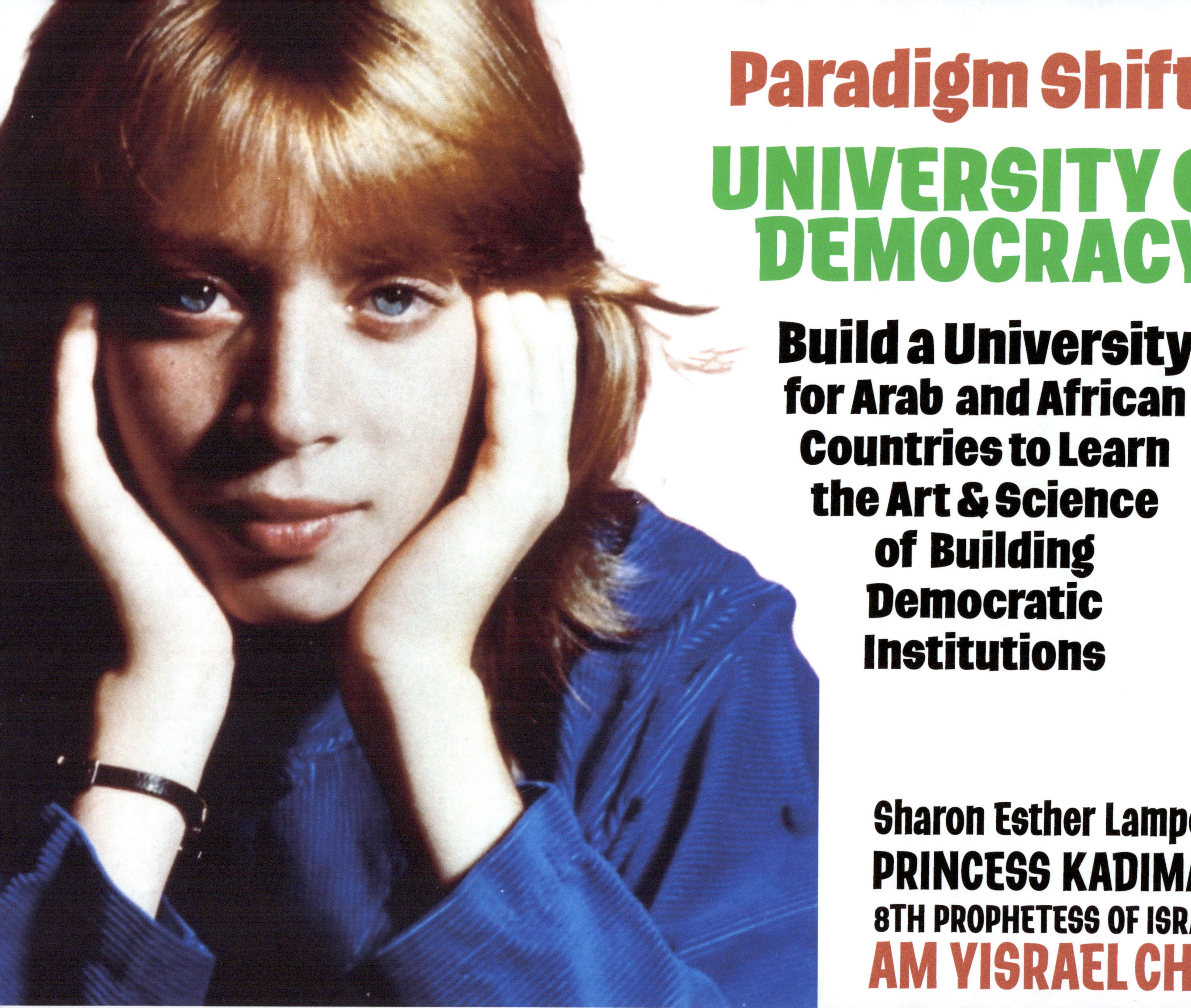

Paradigm Shift 5
UNIVERSITY OF DEMOCRACY
Build a University for Arab and African Countries to Learn the Art & Science of Building Democratic Institutions
Sharon Esther Lampert
PRINCESS KADIMAH
8TH PROPHETESS OF ISRAEL
AM YISRAEL CHAI

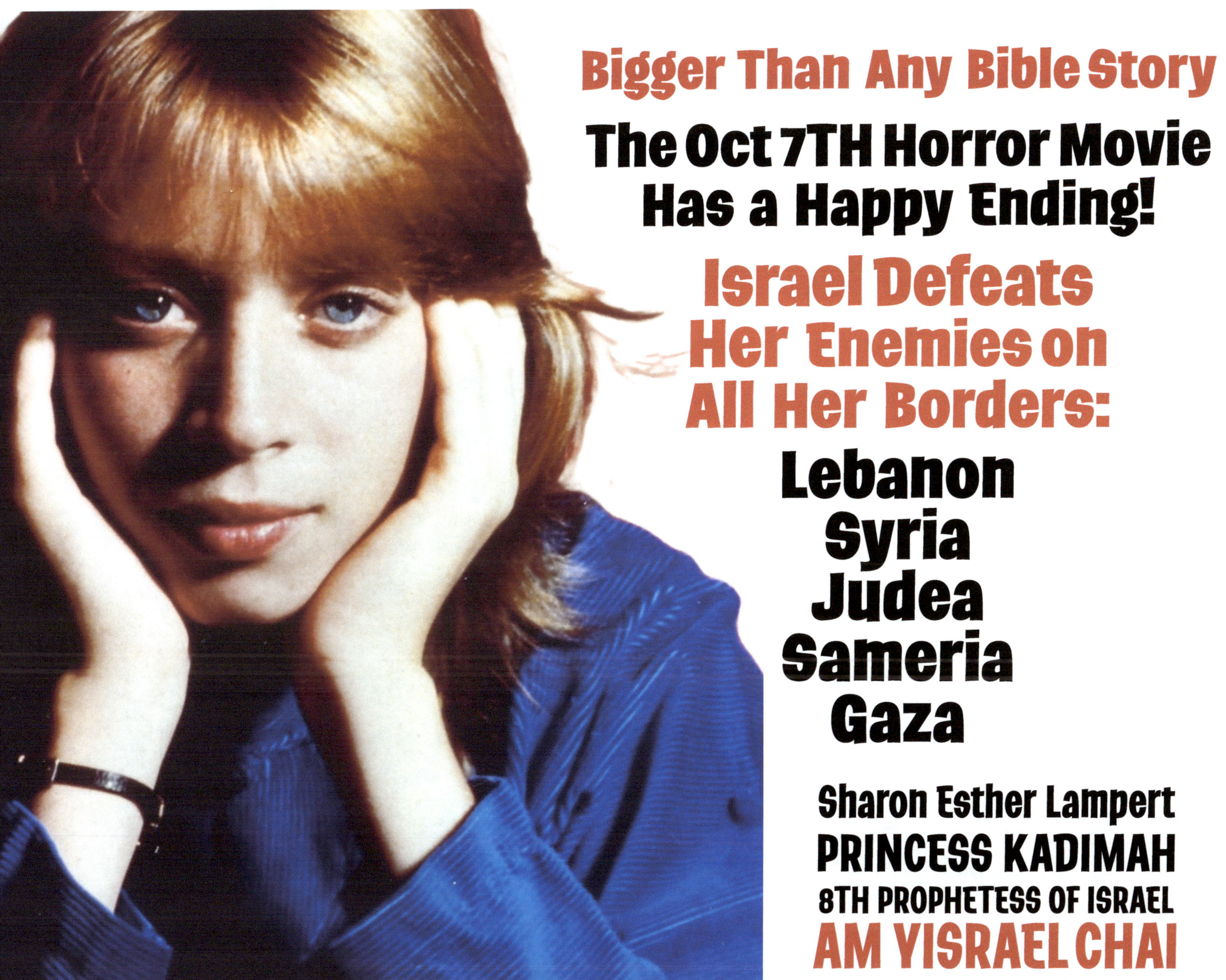

Bigger Than Any Bible Story
The Oct 7TH Horror Movie Has a Happy Ending!
Israel Defeats Her Enemies on All Her Borders:
Lebanon
Syria
Judea
Sameria
Gaza
Sharon Esther Lampert
PRINCESS KADIMAH
8TH PROPHETESS OF ISRAEL
AM YISRAEL CHAI

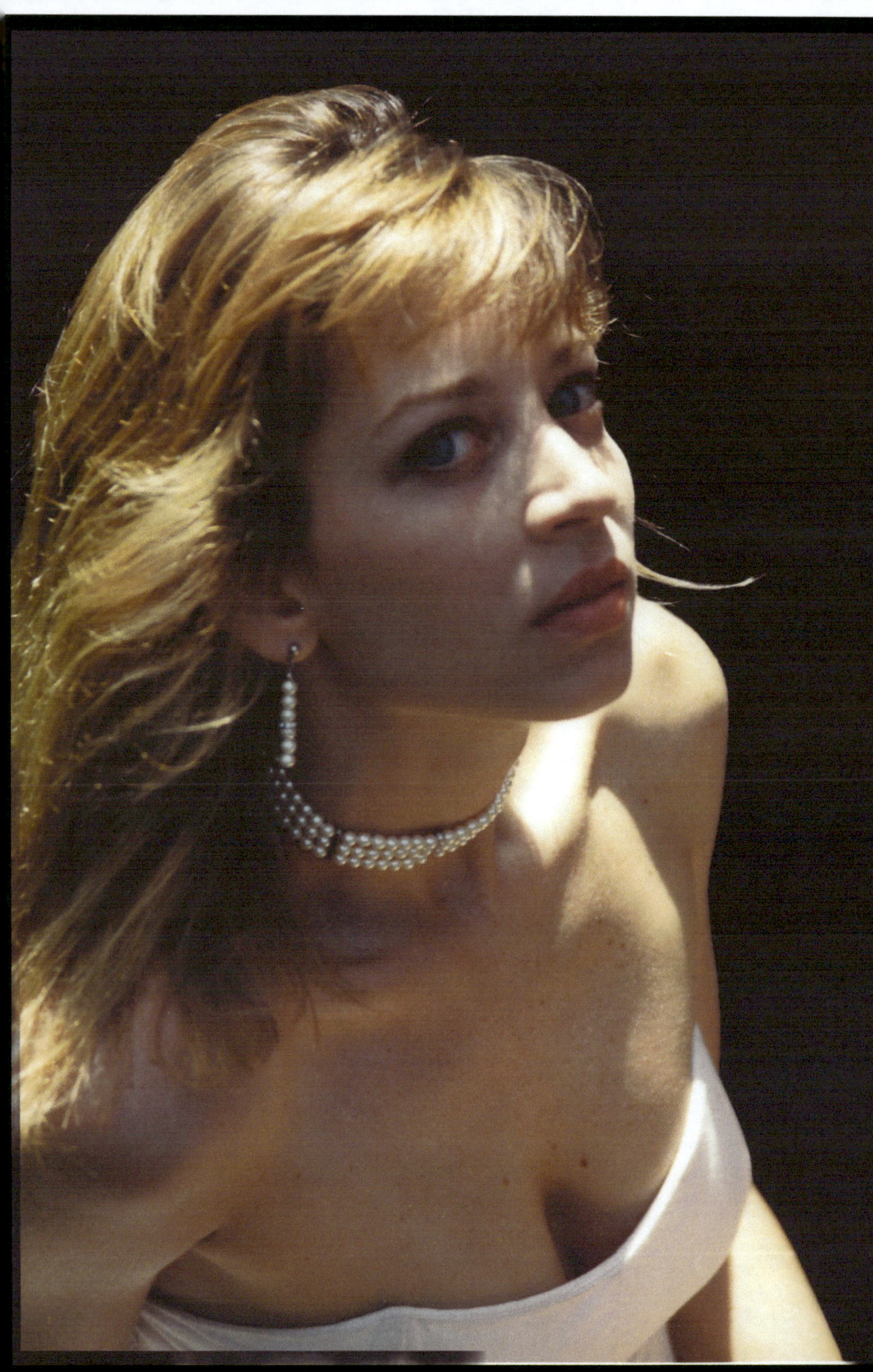

RECONSERVADOX
On Religious Affliation

"I am a ...
RE-CONSERVA-DOX.

I am an amalgum of
Reform, Conservative,
and Orthodox Judaism.

I am the only member
of the group.

It is a great spiritual
challenge.

I have to like everybody!

Sharon Esther Lampert

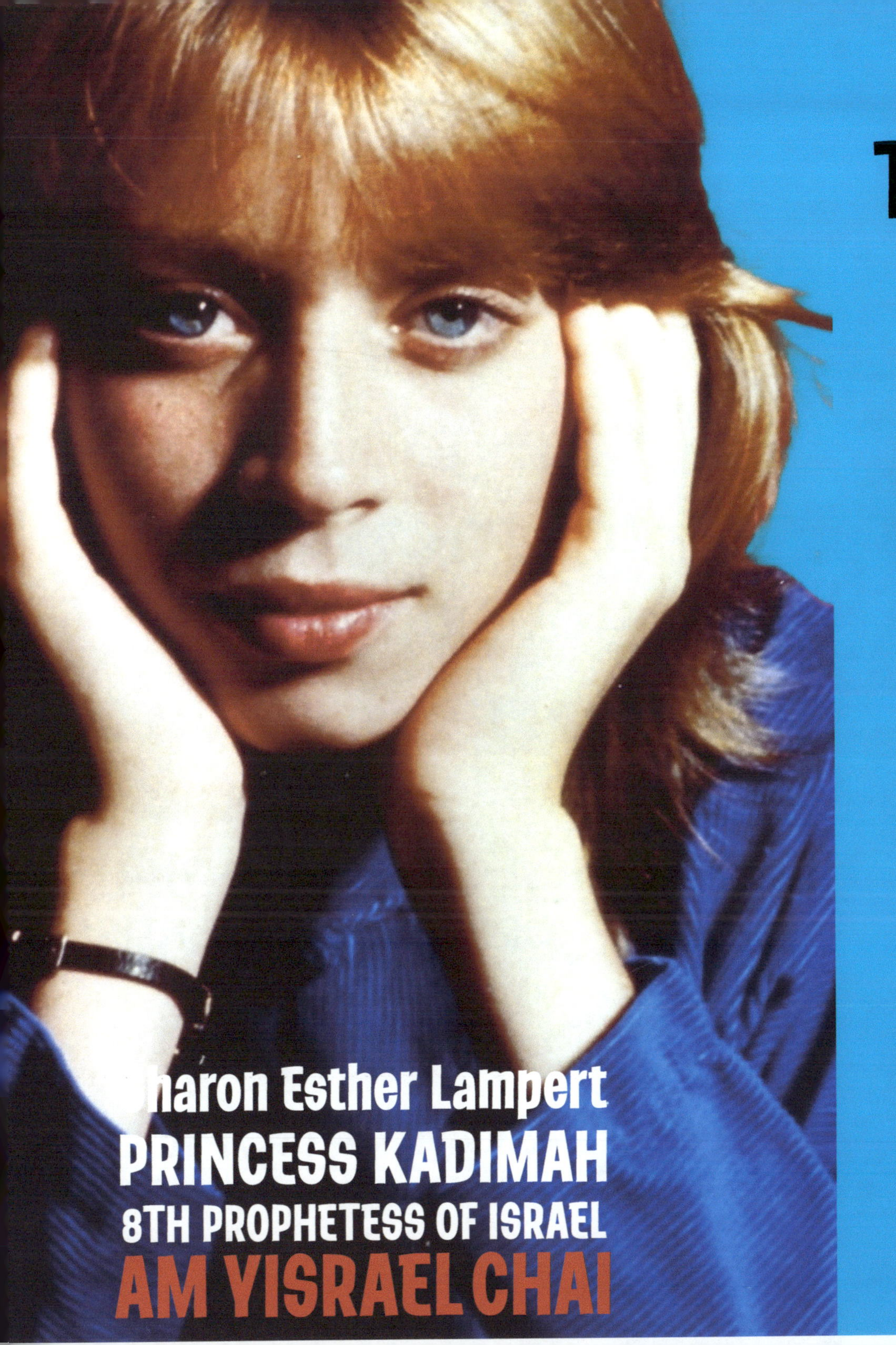

The **worst** thing that has ever happened to me is that I was born.

The **best** thing that has ever happened to me is that I was born **JEWISH**

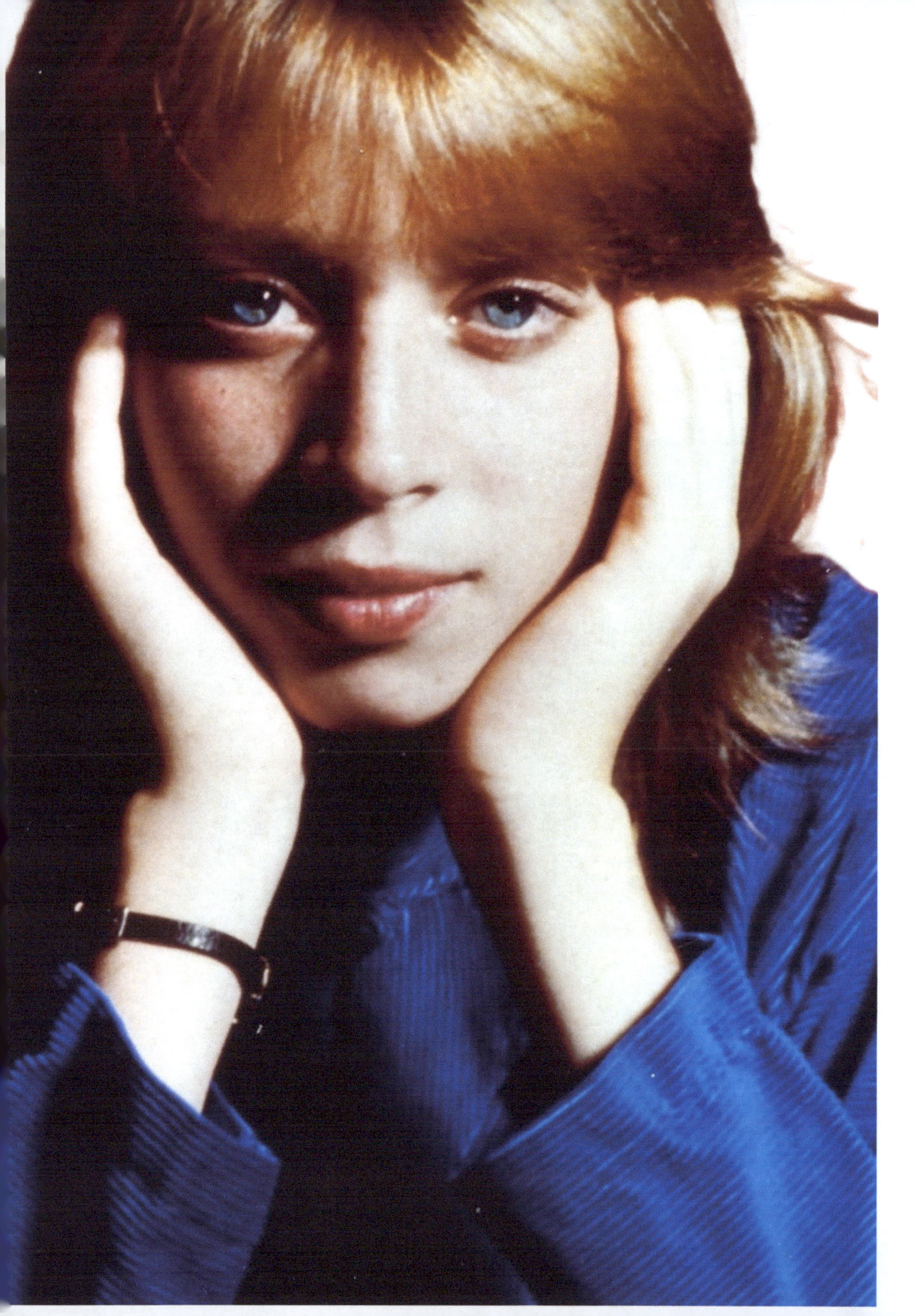

I AM A PROPHET
I deliver the message
What you do with the message is your business!
Sharon Esther Lampert
PRINCESS KADIMAH
8TH PROPHETESS OF ISRAEL
GOD IS GO! DO!
THE 22 COMMANDMENTS

YOU HAD DO OUTDO MOSES

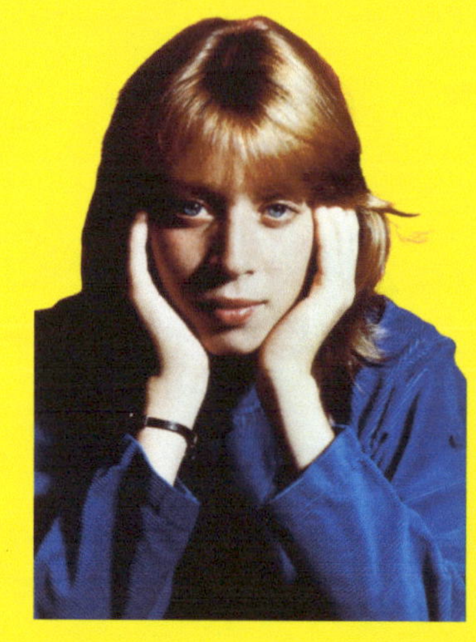

Introducing ...

THE 22 COMMANDMENTS
UNIVERSAL MORAL COMPASS
FOR ALL PEOPLE
FOR ALL RELIGIONS
FOR ALL TIME

ALL YOU WILL EVER NEED TO KNOW ABOUT GOD

THE 22 COMMANDMENTS
UNIVERSAL MORAL COMPASS

1st Commandment: LIFE Over Death
2nd Commandment: STRENGTH Over Weakness
3rd Commandment: DEED Over Sin
4th Commandment: LOVE Over Hatred
5th Commandment: TRUTH Over Lie
6th Commandment: COURAGE Over Fear
7th Commandment: OPTIMISM Over Pessimism
8th Commandment: SHARING Over Selfishness
9th Commandment: PRAISE Over Criticism
10th Commandment: LOYALTY Over Abandonment
11th Commandment: RESPONSIBILITY Over Blame
12th Commandment: GRATITUDE Over Grievances
13th Commandment: REWARD Over Punishment
14th Commandment: DEMOCRACY Over Domination
15th Commandment: CREATION Over Destruction
16th Commandment: EDUCATION Over Ignorance
17th Commandment: COOPERATION Over Competition
18th Commandment: FREEDOM Over Oppression
19th Commandment: COMPASSION Over Indifference
20th Commandment: FORGIVENESS Over Revenge
21st Commandment: PEACE Over War
22nd Commandment: JOY Over Suffering

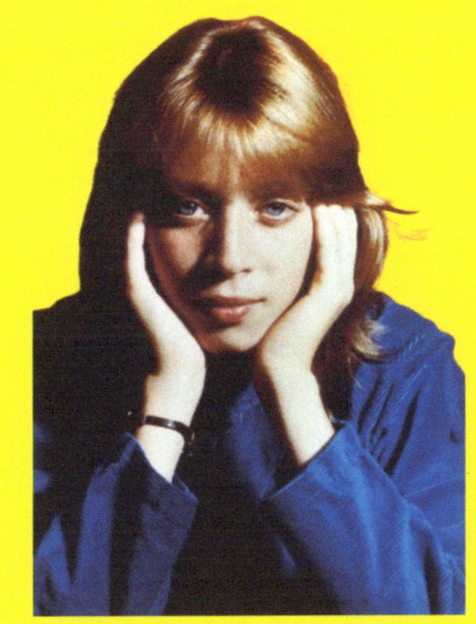

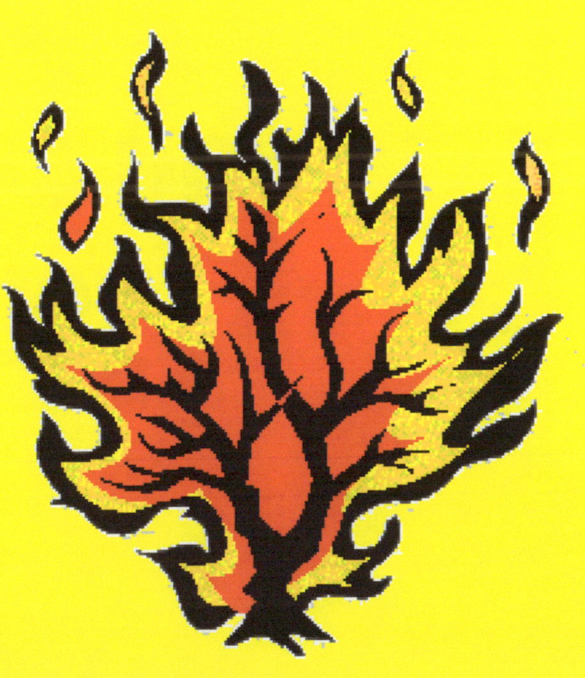

Prophet Sharon Esther Lampert

BE ART
ART IS SMART
ART IS FROM THE HEART
MAKE ART NOT WAR
YOU ARE BORN FOR GREATNESS
YOU ARE A MASTERPIECE
Sharon Esther Lampert

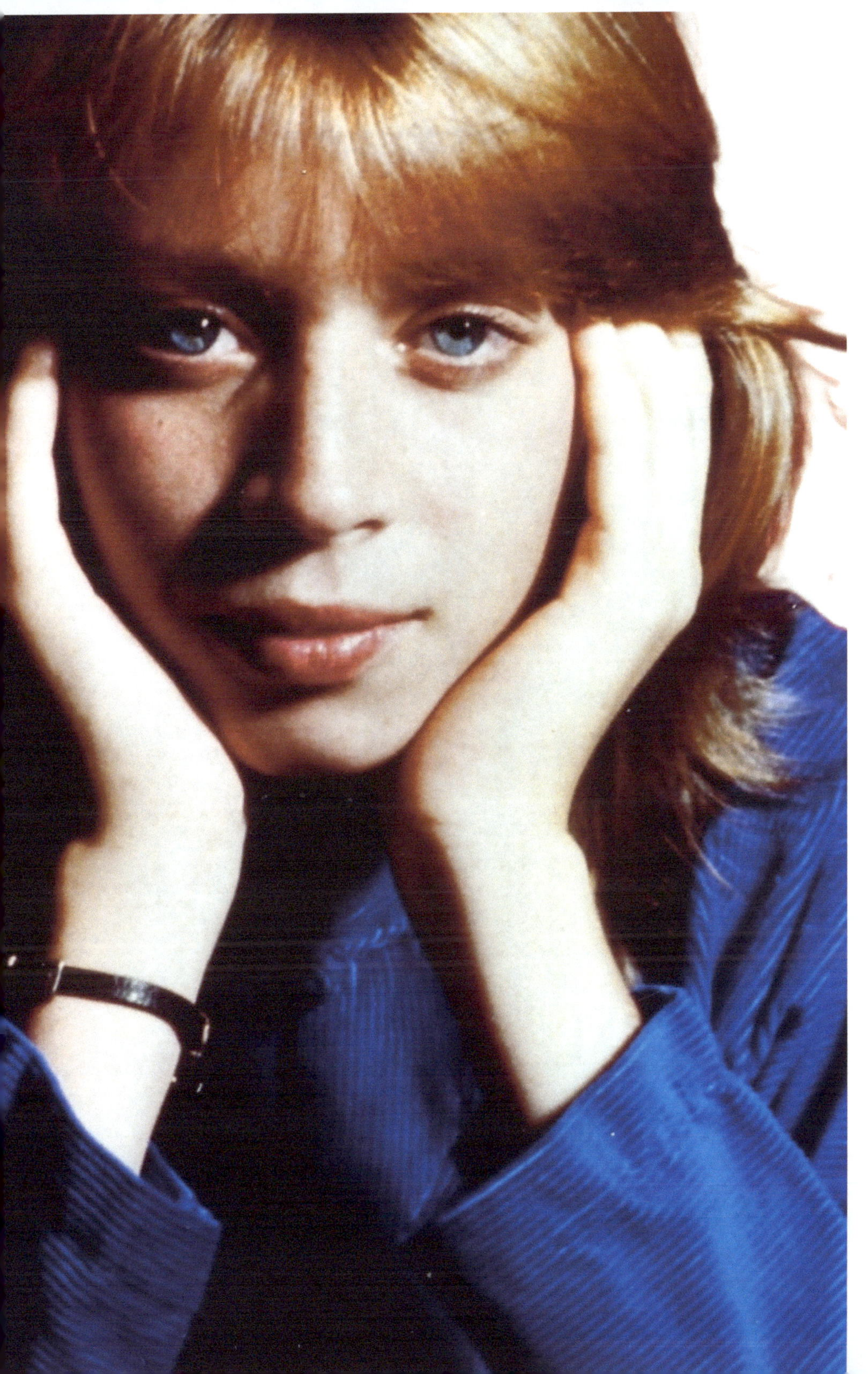

BEZALEL

Artistic Gifts Are Inherited.
My Father's Nickname Was **BEZALEL** I Inherited the **BLESSING!**

EXODUS 31:3

Then the Lord said to Moses: "See, I have chosen **BEZALEL** son of Uri, the son of Hur, of the tribe of Judah and I have filled him with the **SPIRIT OF GOD**, with wisdom, with understanding with knowledge, and with all kinds of skills.

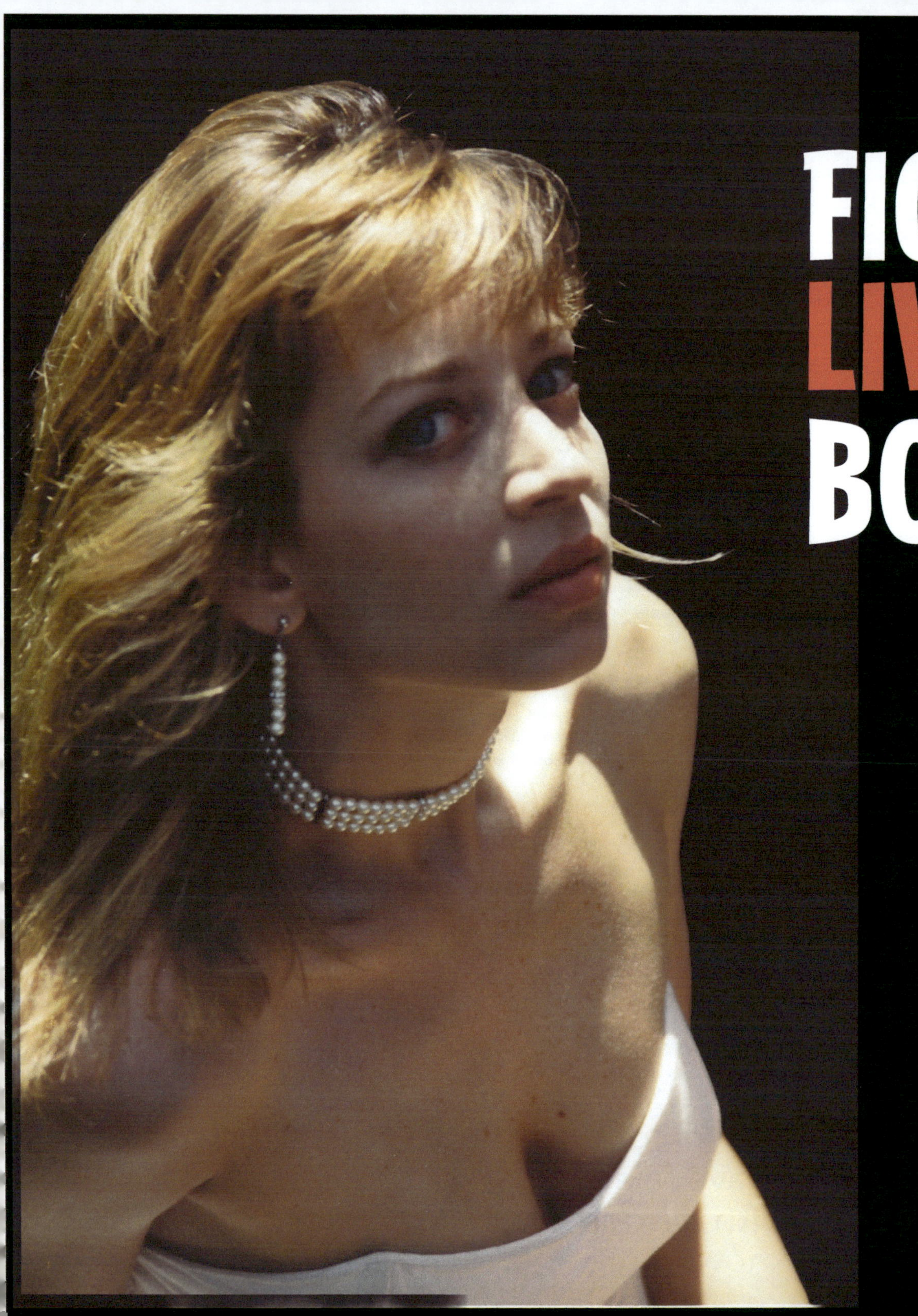

FIGHT TO LIVE
LIVE TO FIGHT
BORN TO DIE

SHARON
ESTHER
LAMPERT

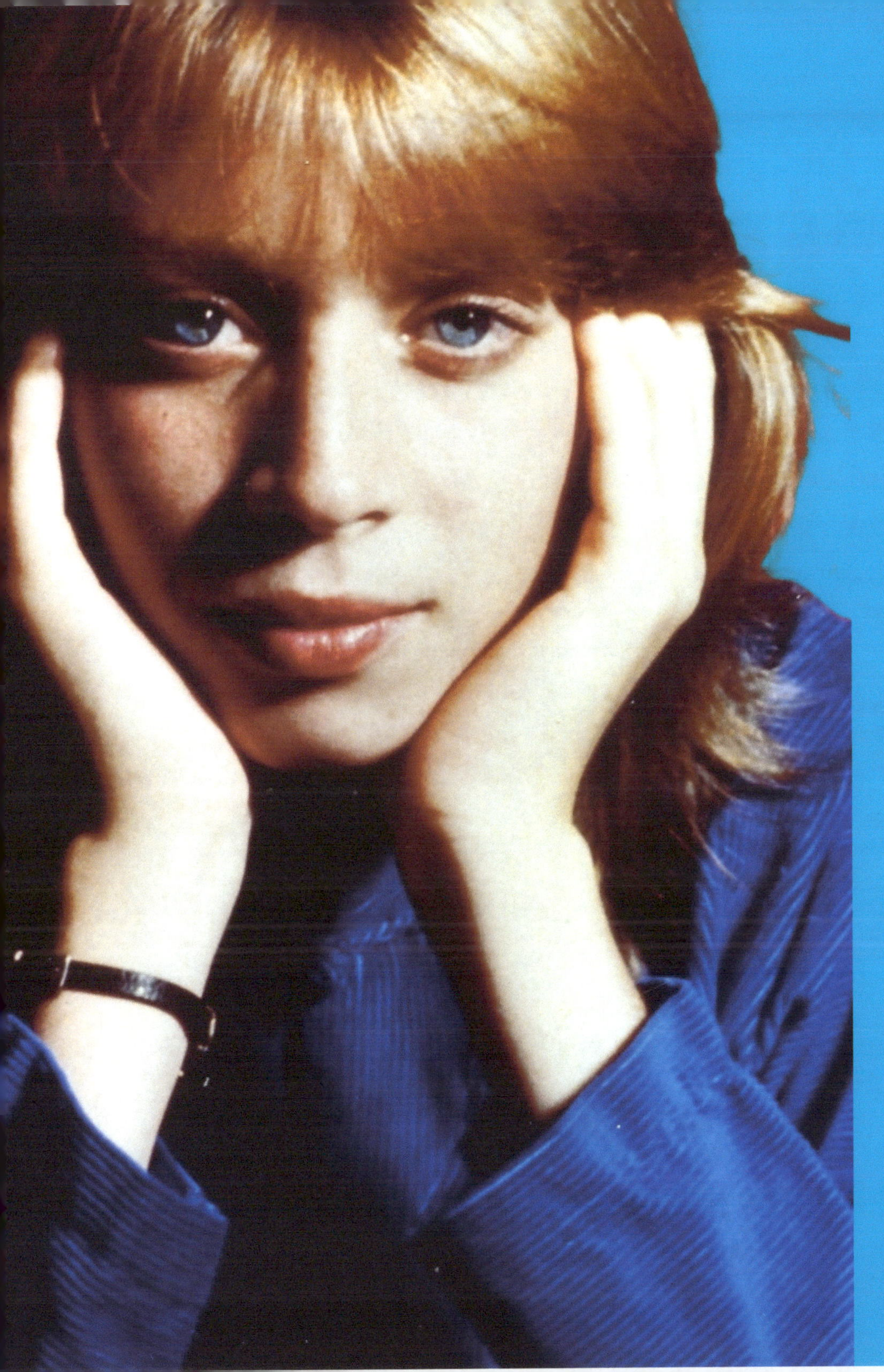

FIGHT TO LIVE
LIVE TO FIGHT
BORN TO DIE

Sharon Esther Lampert

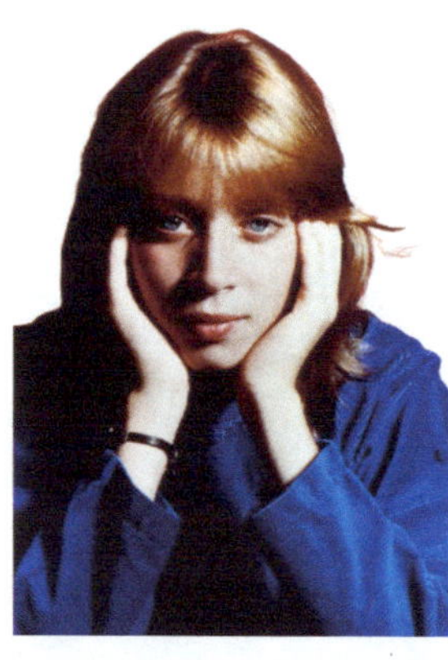

Sharon Esther Lampert

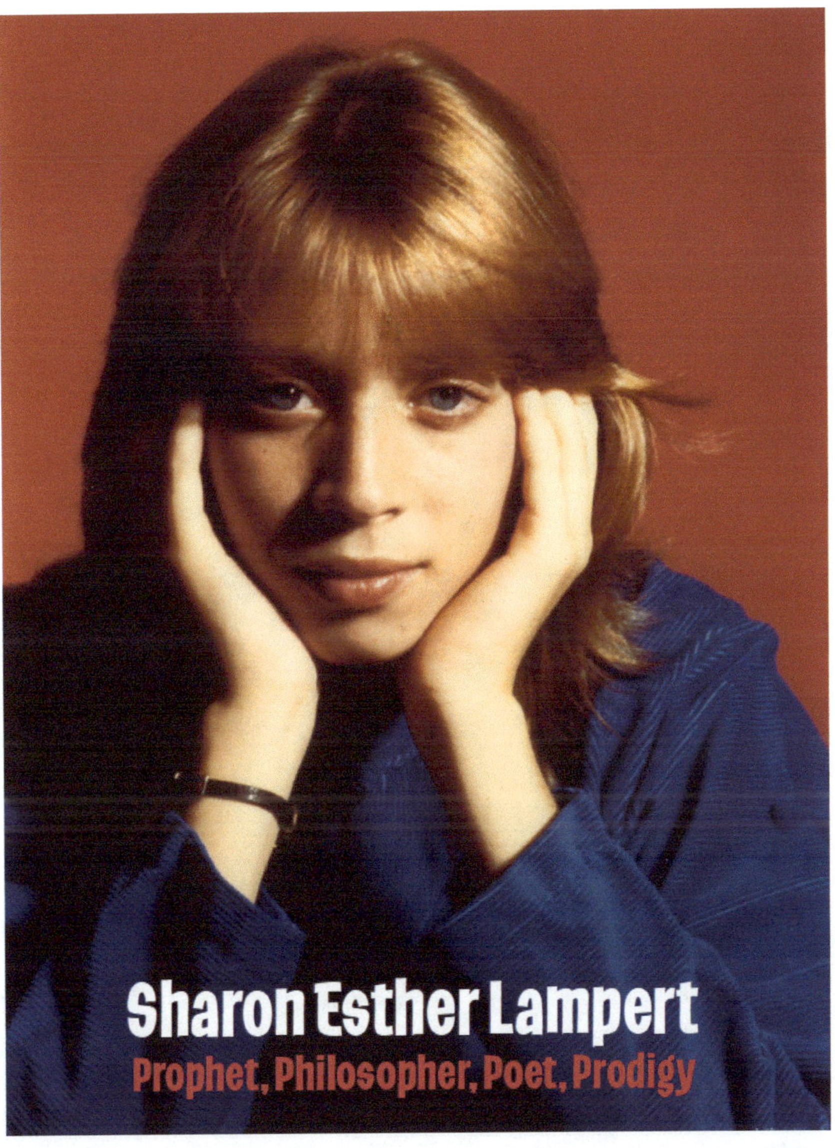

NO FAKES
NO FLOPS
NO FILLER
NO FLUFF
NO FUDGE
NO FAT
NO F-BOMB

©SharonEstherLampert.com

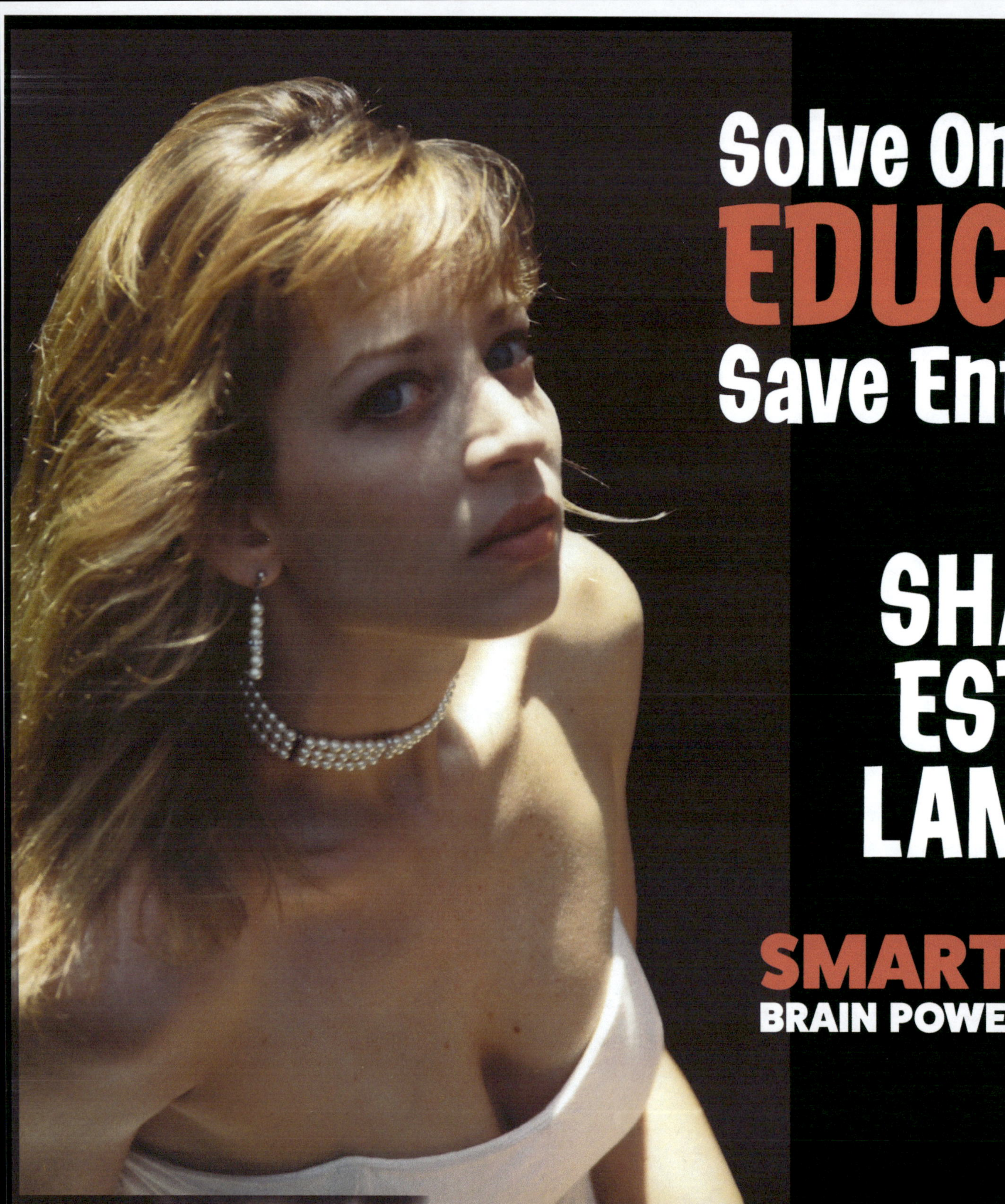

Solve One Problem
EDUCATION
Save Entire World
SHARON
ESTHER
LAMPERT
SMARTGRADES
BRAIN POWER REVOLUTION

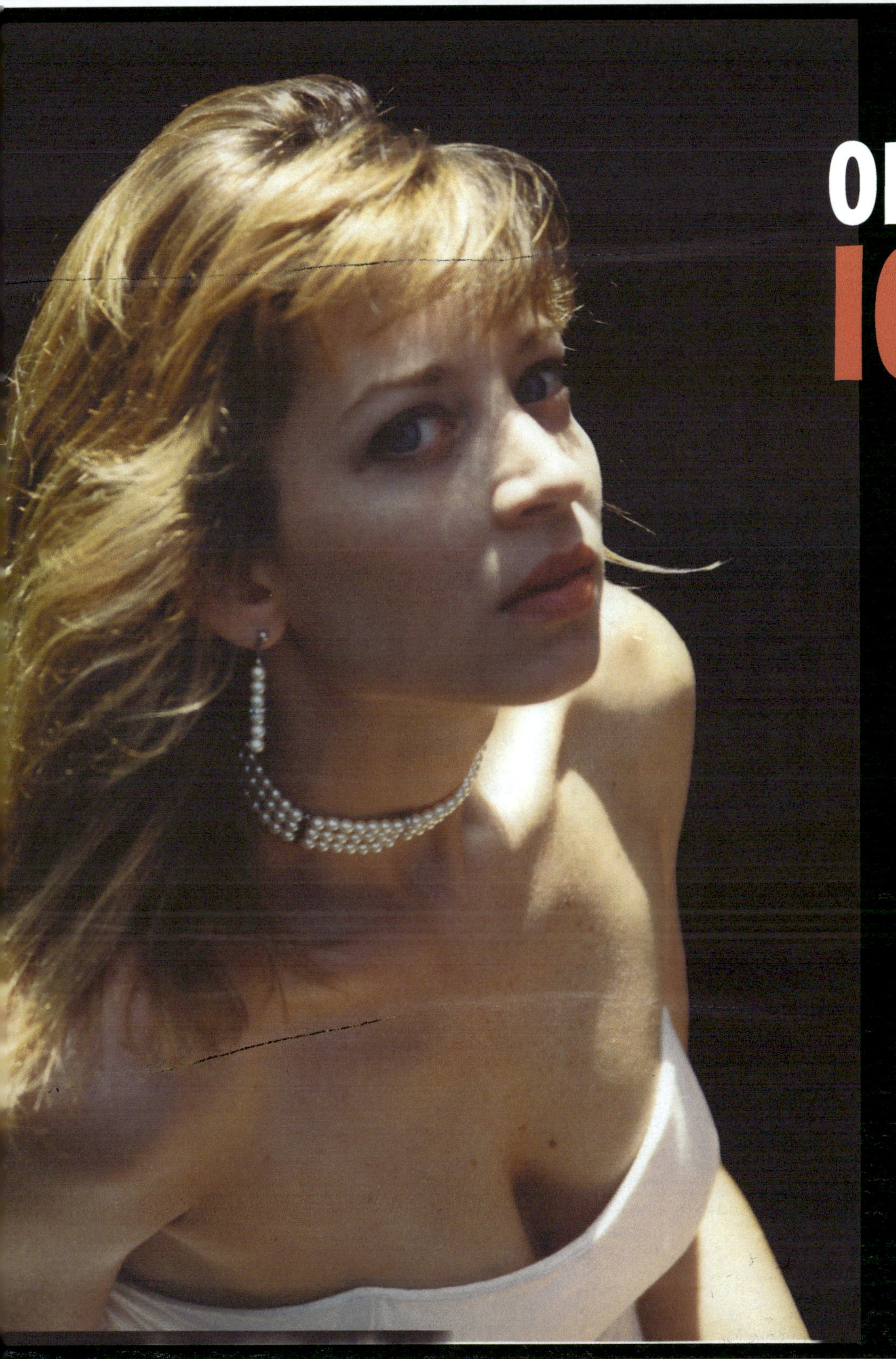

ONE GLOBAL ENEMY
IGNORANCE

SHARON
ESTHER
LAMPERT

SMARTGRADES
BRAIN POWER REVOLUTION

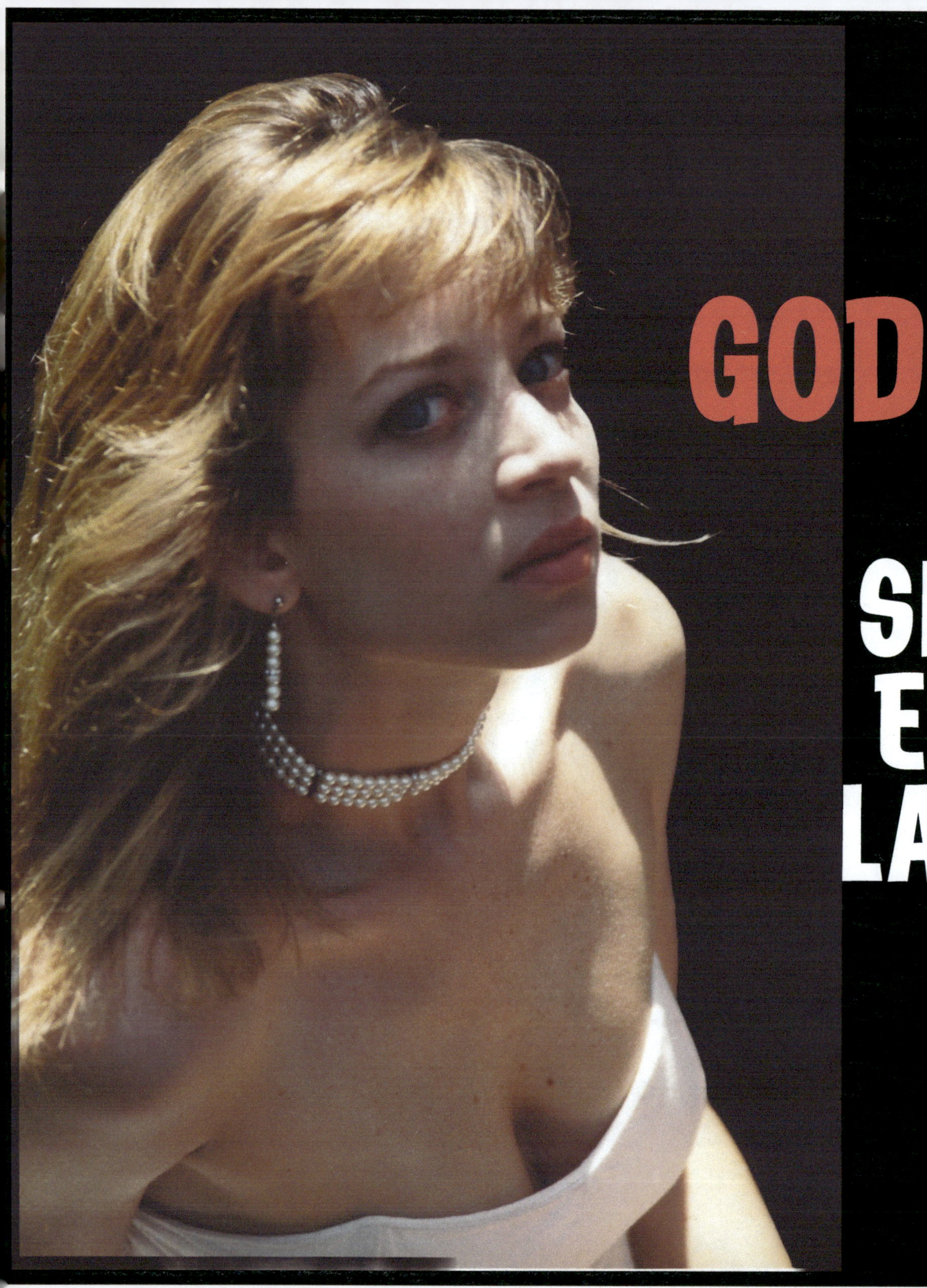

GOD IS GO! DO!

SHARON
ESTHER
LAMPERT

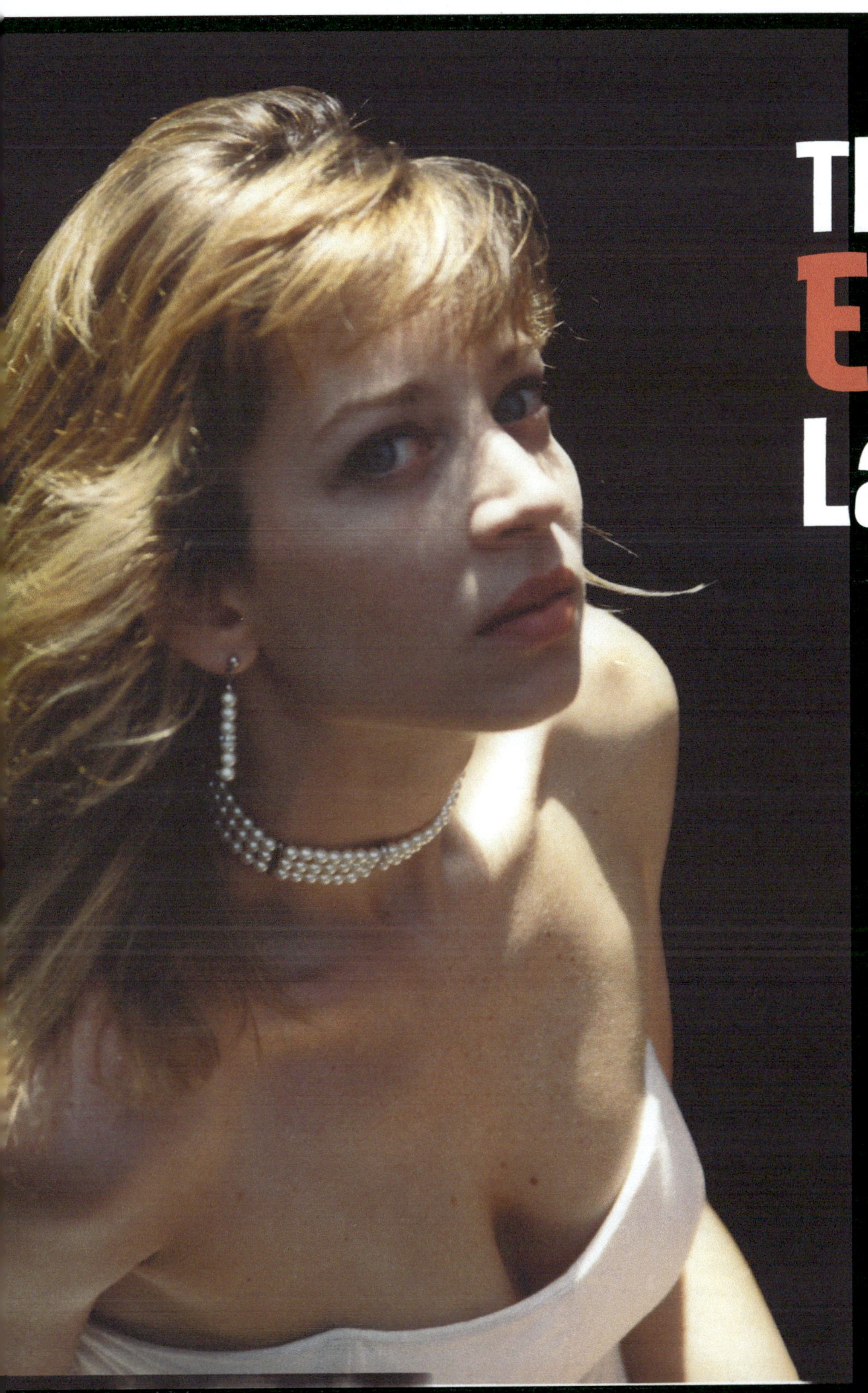

The First Steps In
EDUCATION
Last a Lifetime

SHARON
ESTHER
LAMPERT

SMARTGRADES
BRAIN POWER REVOLUTION

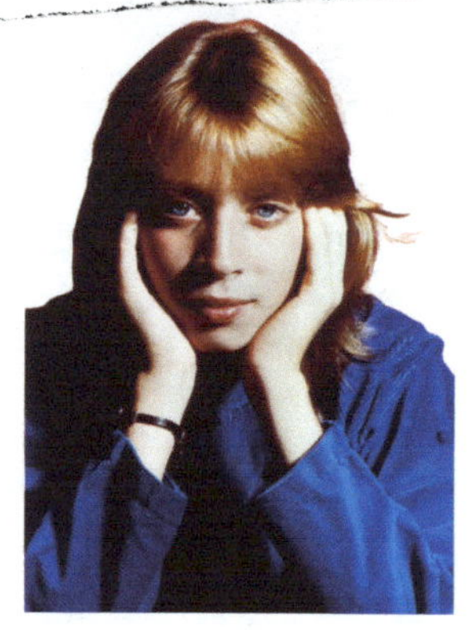

TRUE LOVE

True Love Is Unconditional
True Love Is Found in the Deed
True Love Is Found in the We
True Love Joins the Heart
Mind, and Body as One

Sharon Esther Lampert

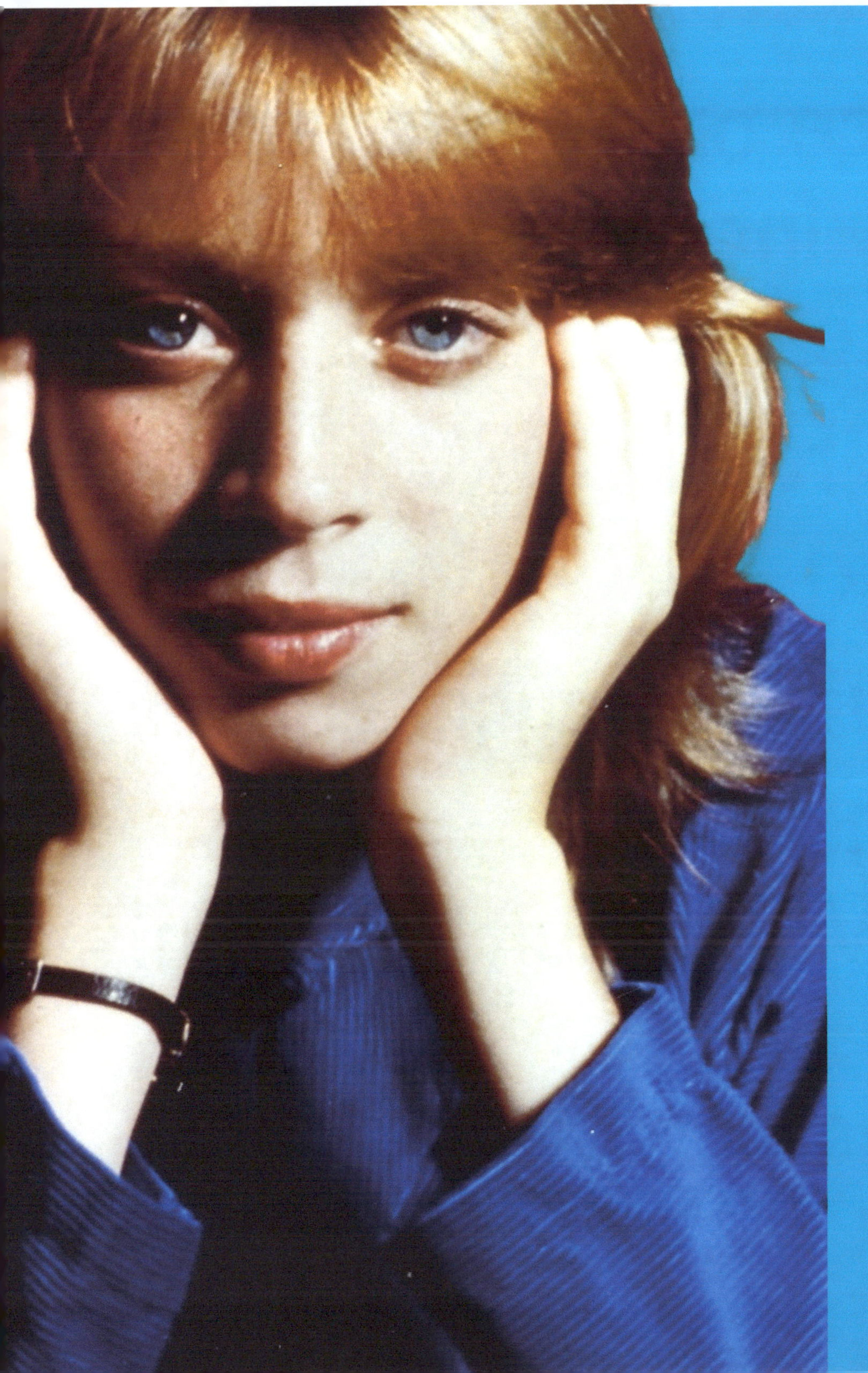

Do you
want me
to sign it
in
INK
or
in
LIPSTICK?
Sharon Esther Lampert

All Writers Write on Blank Pages
Turning NOTHING into SOMETHING.
All Writers Write the Exact Same
Way: ONE WORD AT A TIME!
WRITERS RUN THE WORLD
Books, Movies, Songs, Prayers, Jokes
LAST WILL and TESTAMENT
Please Don't Let Me Die with a Typo!

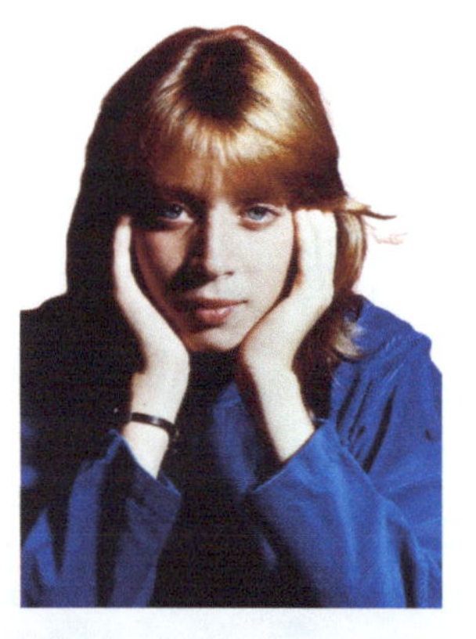

Sharon Esther Lampert

SEE THE WORLD THROUGH THE EYES OF A CREATIVE GENIUS

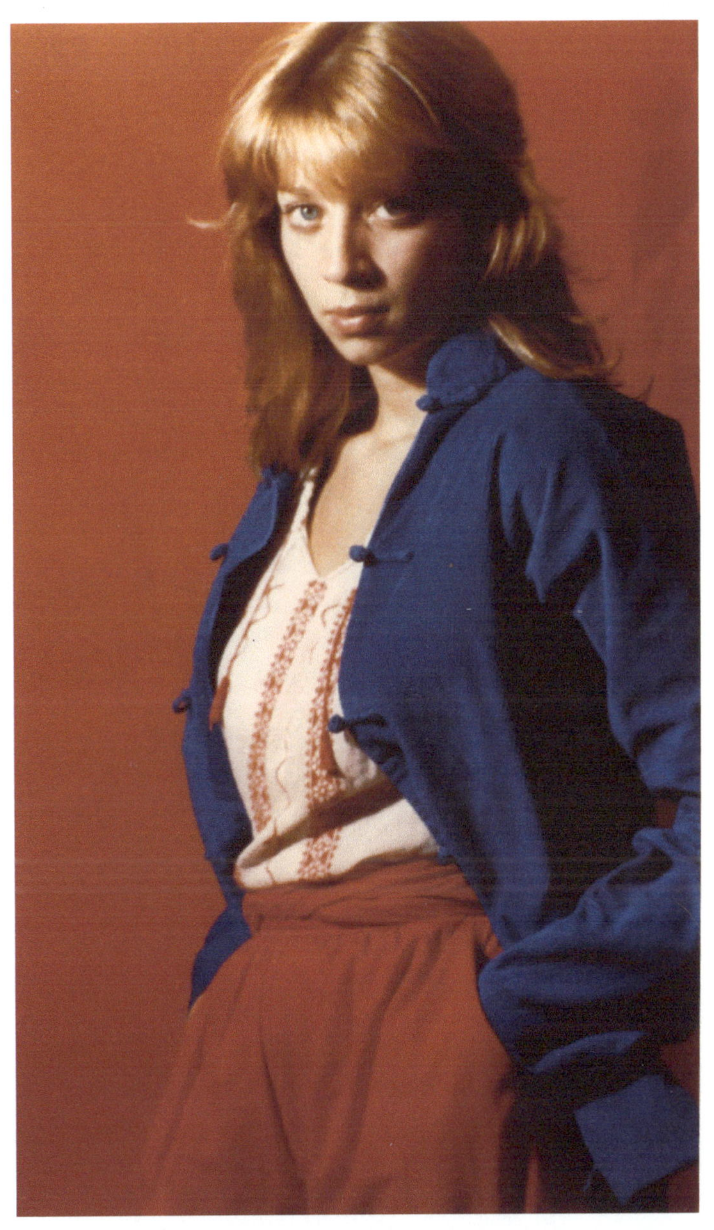

WARNING

KEEP A SAFE DISTANCE OF 6 FEET

HIGH LEVELS OF INTENSITY
INTELLECTUAL COMBUSTION

SHARON ESTHER LAMPERT

PRODIGY

**POET, PHILOSOPHER, PROPHET, PEACEMAKER,
PALADIN OF EDUCATION, PHOTON SUPERHERO
PIONEER, PERFORMER, PUBLISHER, PLAYER
PRESIDENT, PHOENIX, PRINCESS of ISRAEL**

www.SharonEstherLampert.com
FANS@sharonestherlampert.com

What Happens When You Dress Up Albert Einstein As Marilyn Monroe?

SHARON ESTHER LAMPERT

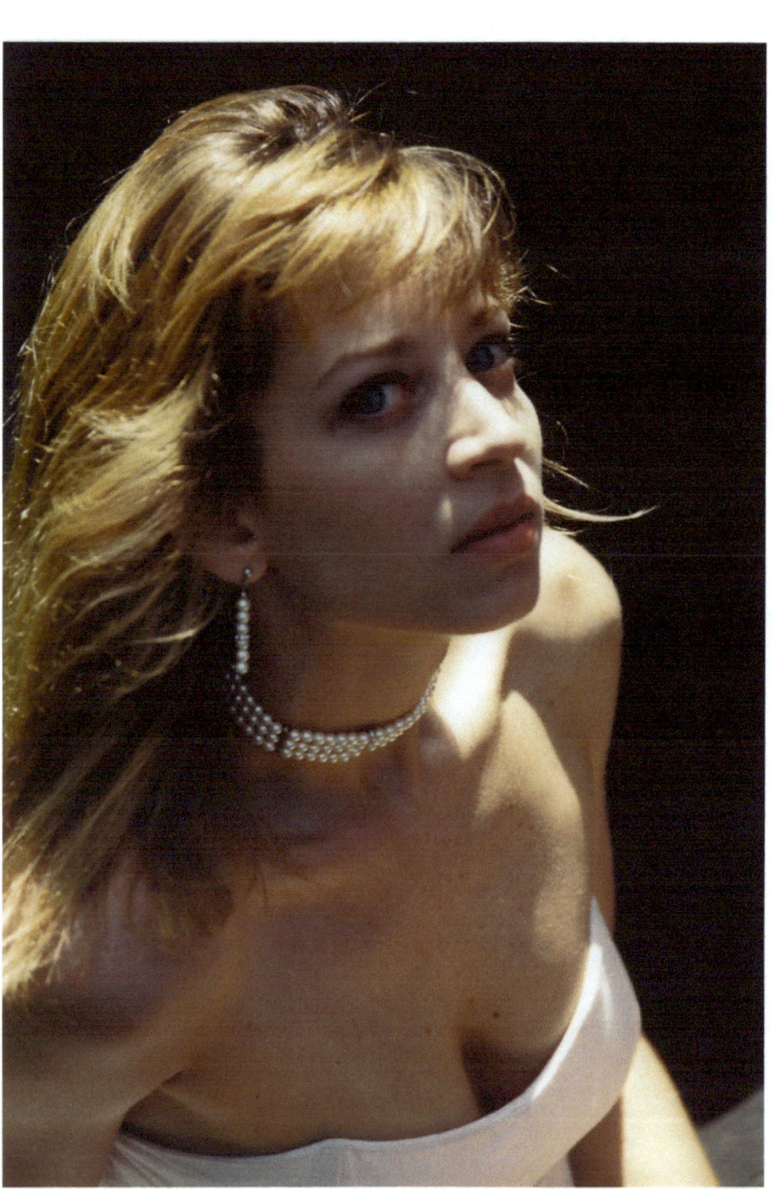

- Prodigy
- Poet
- Prophet
- Philosopher
- Peacemaker
- Paladin of Education
- **PHOTON SUPERHERO**
- Princess KADIMAH
- Princess & Pea
- Performer: Vocalist
- Player: Jock NYU Varsity B-Ball
- President
- Publisher
- Producer
- Psychobiologist:Rockefeller University
- Piano-Playing Cat
- Phoenix
- **PINUP**

WEBSITES
- SharonEstherLampert.com
- WorldFamousPoems.com
- PoetryJewels.com
- PhilosopherQueen.com
- GodIsGoDo.com
- Schmaltzy.com
- TrueLoveBurnsEternal.com
- SillyLittleBoys.com
- WinAtThin.com
- WritersRunTheWorld.com
- PalmBeachBookPublisher.com
- BooksArePowerful.com
- HappyGrandparenting.com
- WomenHaveAllThePower.com

EDUCATION
- Smartgrades.com
- PhotonSuperHero.com
- EveryDayAnEasyA.com
- BooksNotBombs.com

NYU
AWARD for Multi-Interdisciplinary Studies

SHARON IS HERE THERE AND EVERYWHERE

The **IDEA** of Sharon Esther Lampert was born in ISRAEL. For Sharon to be born, her mother and father traveled to **ISRAEL,** met, and married. Abraham Lampert survived the Holocaust, and came to Israel on the boat **AP AL PI CHEN** (Haifa Museum) For two years, he was detained in Cyprus camps. He lived in Israel for 10 years. Her mother and father spoke to each other in Yiddish with Russian-Jewish backgrounds. Four languages were spoken at home: English, Hebrew, Yiddish, and Russian.

Honors & Awards

NYU AWARD
Multi-Interdisciplinary Studies
NYU 3 Degrees: BA, MA, MA
NYU Varsity Basketball Team
NYU Weightlifting Contest

NYC AWARD
100 Year Scholarship Award
Presented by NYC Mayor Koch

NY EMPIRE STATE AWARD
Math and Science Scholarship

JERUSALEM FELLOWSHIP
Aish Hatorah, Israel

ROCKEFELLER UNIVERSITY
Science Paper Publication

FIRST PRIZE
Upper East Side Resident
Newspaper Writing Contest

FIRST PRIZE
THE WAVE (1893) Art Contest

#1 POETRY WEBSITE
For Student Poetry Projects

POETRY WORLD RECORD
120 Words of Rhyme from
One Family of Rhyme

CONTRIBUTIONS TO CIVILIZATION
Scientist, Artist, Educator, Theologian

Published 80+ Books
NYU: PERSTARE et PRAESTARE

PRODIGY
10 Esoteric Laws of Genius and Creativity
Awesome Art of Alliteration Using One Letter of the Alphabet

PROPHET
GOD IS GO! DO!
22 COMMANDMENTS: A UNIVERSAL MORAL COMPASS

PHYSICIST
LAWS OF INEXTRICABILITY - NEW SCIENTIFIC THEORY!

PSYCHOBIOLOGIST
THE SPERM MANIFESTO: 10 RULES FOR THE ROAD - - NEW SCIENTIFIC THEORY!

PHILOSOPHER QUEEN
The Philosophy of Love: ME & WE
The Philosophy of Evil: THE DOUBLE WHAMMY
Women Have All The Power But Have Never Learned How to Use It

POET
WORLD POETRY RECORD **120 Words of Rhyme from One Family of Rhyme**
#1 Poetry Website for Student Projects
The Greatest Poems Ever Written on Extraordinary World Events
The First Woman to Write a Book on 5000 Years of Jewish History

PALADIN OF EDUCATION
SMARTGRADES BRAIN POWER REVOLUTION
8 Goalposts of Education
40 Universal Gold Standards of Education
SCHMALTZY: The First Book of Color-Coded Words
Learn to Read Hebrew in One Hour

PSYCHIATRIST
LOVE YOU MORE THAN YESTERDAY: 14 Relationship Strategies for Happily Ever After
Integration Therapy to Rebuild the Broken Wings of Students
40 RULES OF MANHOOD
3 Stages of Child Abuse

PEACEMAKER
WORLD PEACE EQUATION

PINUP
SEXIEST GENIUS IN HUMAN HISTORY

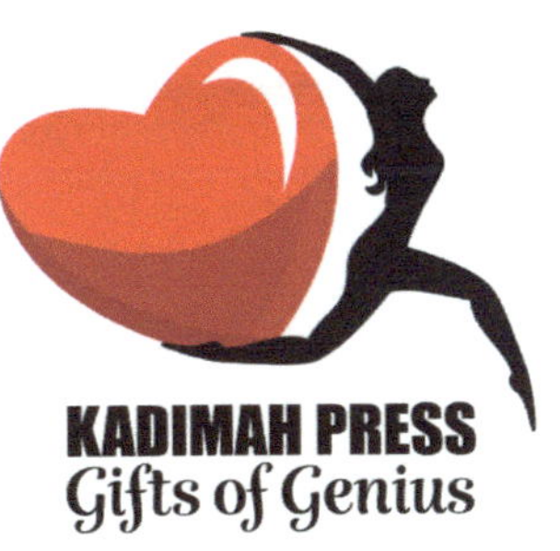

Flunked History

Sitting All Day on Their Ass on the College Grass

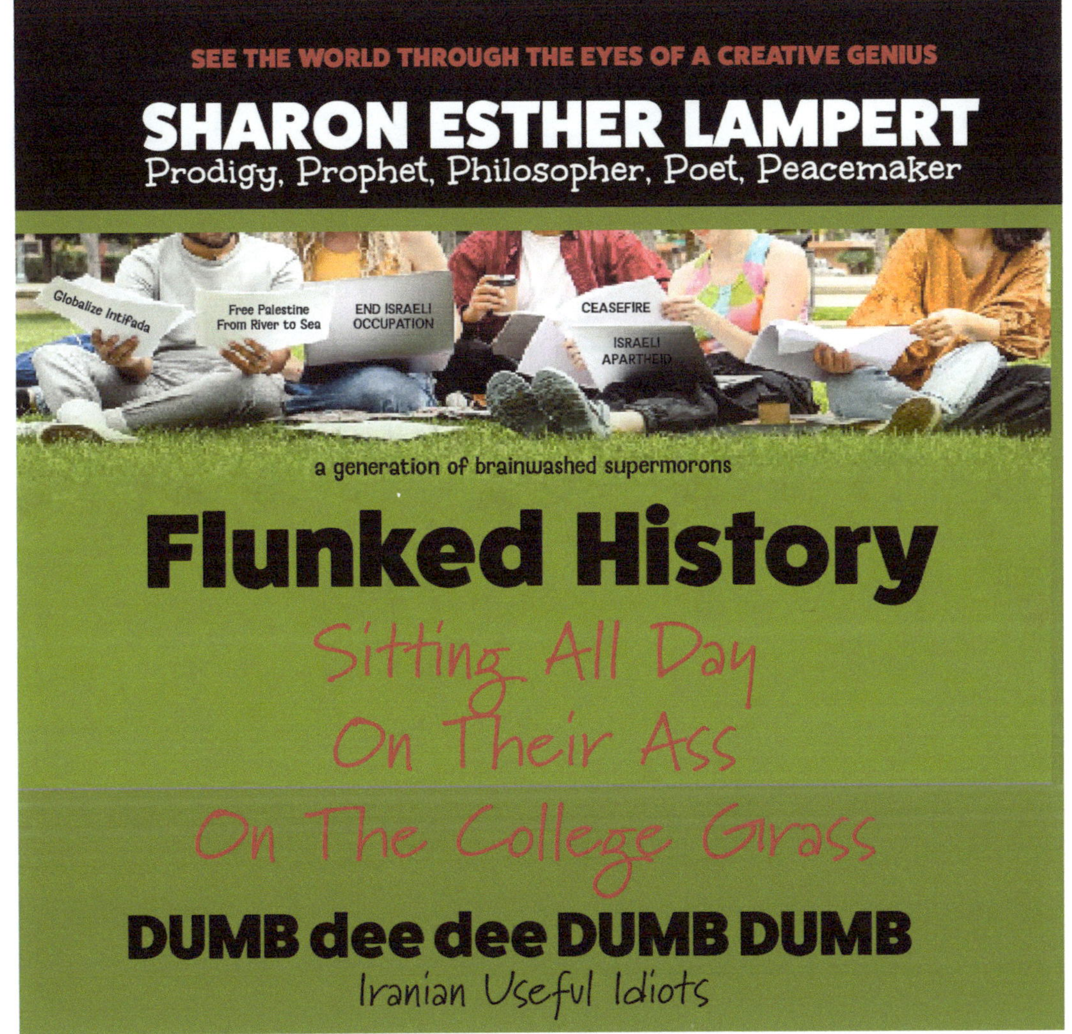

3 Editions:
ISBN Hardcover: 979-8-3482-2802-6
ISBN Paperback: 979-8-3482-9125-9
ISBN e-book: 979-8-3482-9126-6
Library of Congress: 2025900090

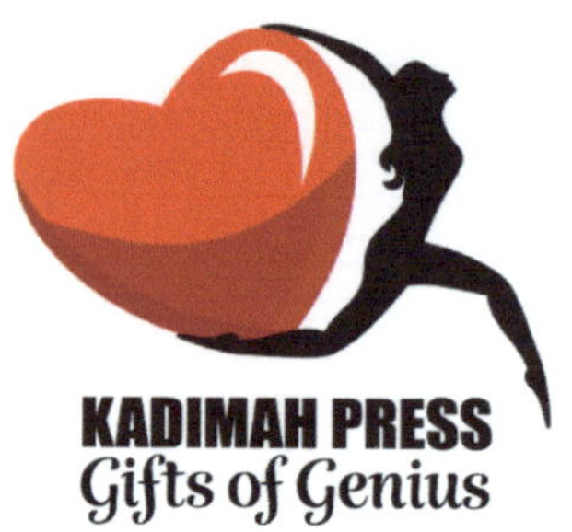

MANY JEWS RECLAIMED GOD

Sharon Esther Lampert Is The **First Women** to Write a Book on 5000 Years of Jewish History

6
POETIC
REFRAINS

First Edition: 1998
Israel's 50TH Anniversary
Update: 75TH Year Anniversary
Update: October 7, 2023

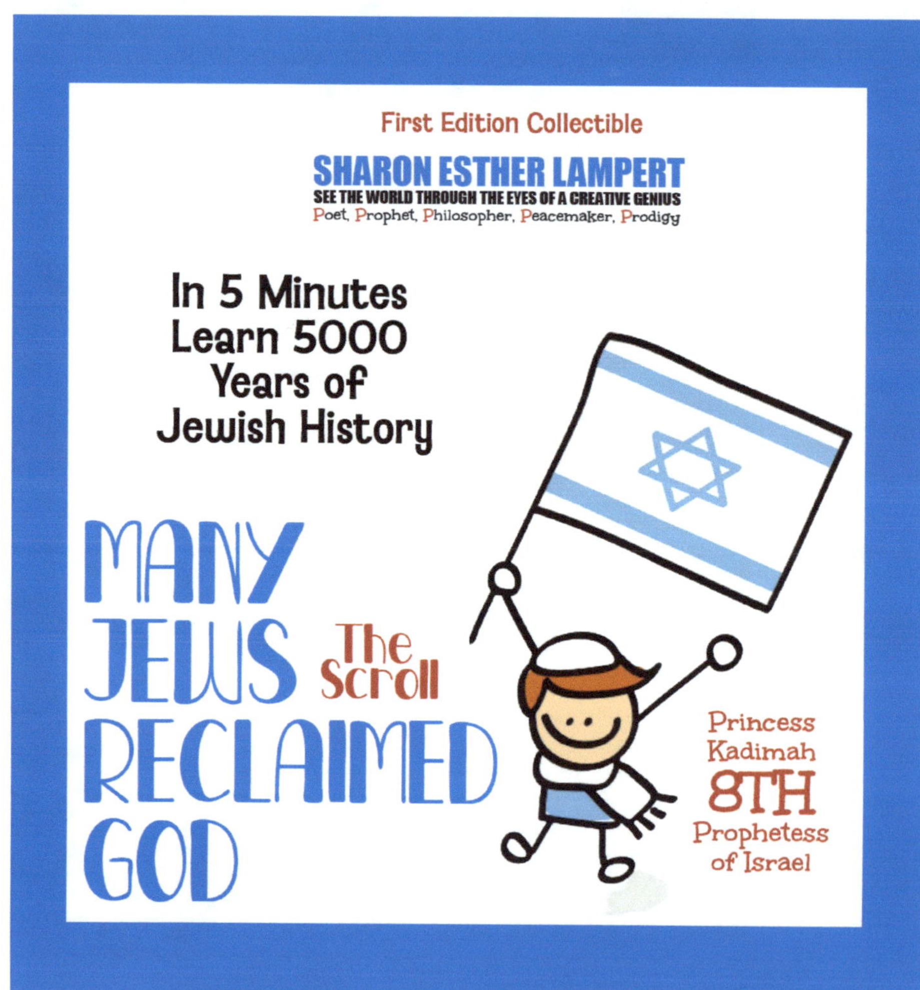

In
5 Minutes
Learn
5000 Years
of
Jewish
History

3 Editions:
ISBN Hardcover: 979-8-8690-79-27-5
ISBN Paperback: 979-8-8690-79-31-2
ISBN e-book: 979-8-8690-79-28-2
Library of Congress: 2024900329

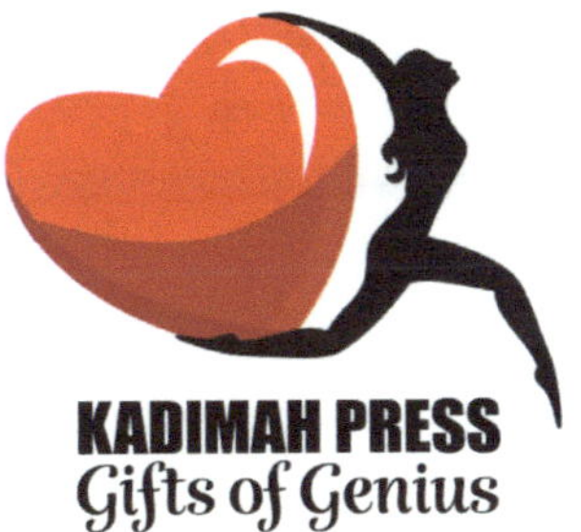

17 HOURS

Israeli Women Warriors of Valor Defeat Evil

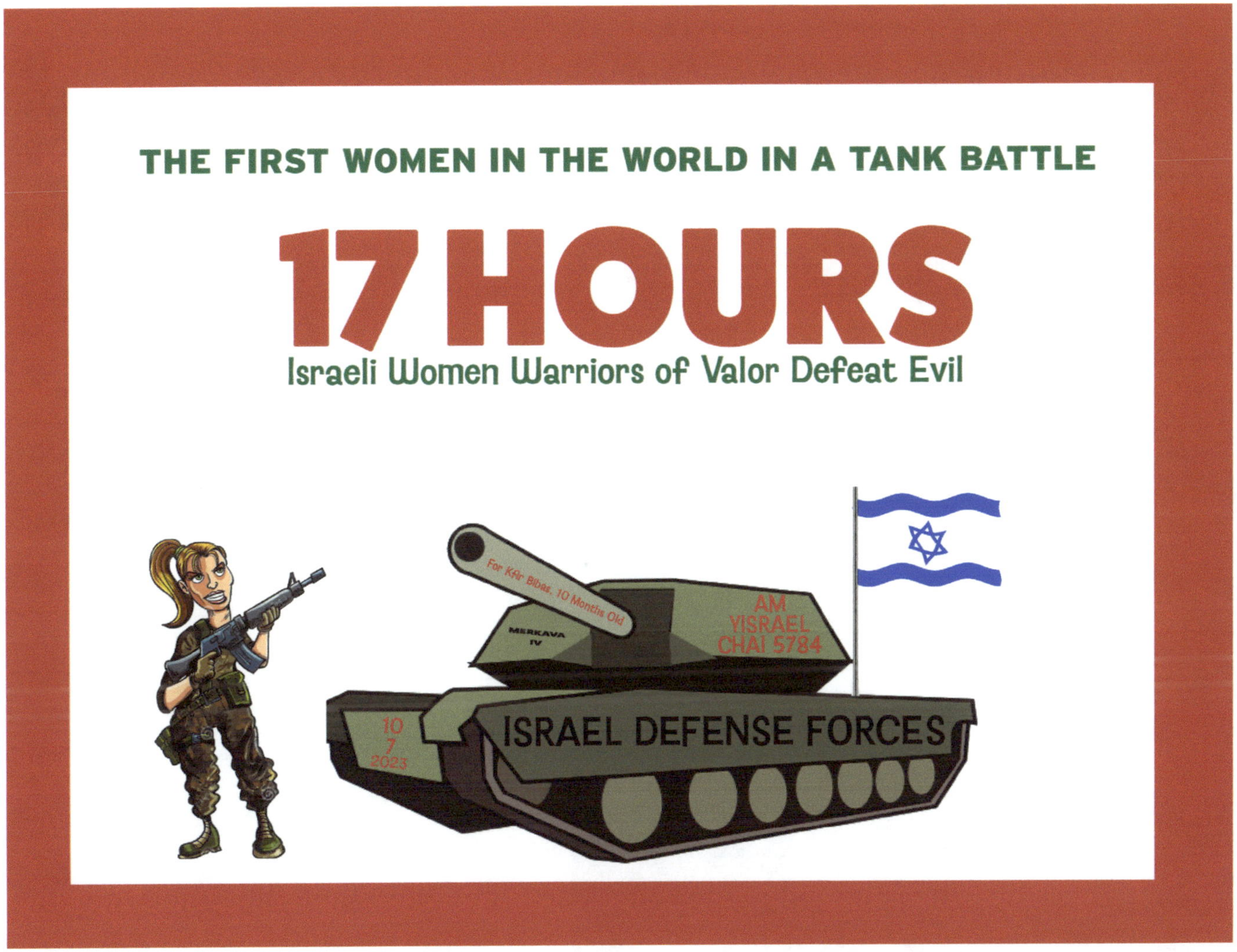

3 Editions:
Hardcover ISBN: 979-8-3482-7996-7
Paperback ISBN: 979-8-3482-8015-4
e-book ISBN: 979-8-3482-8016-1
Library of Congress: 2025927748

My Father Abraham Lampert's Nickname Was

BEZALEL
"In the Shadow of God"

The Chief Architect of the Covenant
I Inherited the Blessing.
Exodus: 31:3

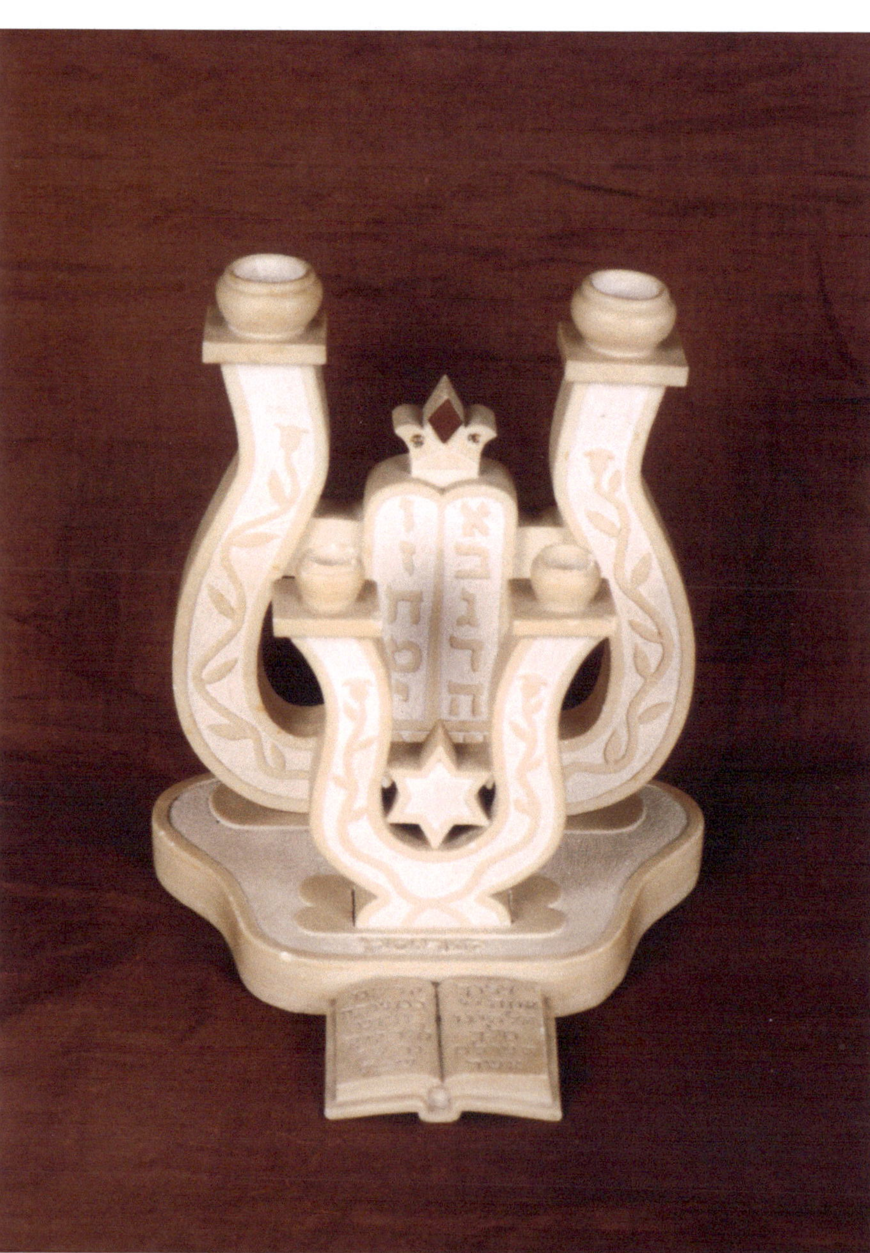

By **Abraham Lampert**
Shabbat Candlesticks Made of Cyprus Stone
Made in the Cyprus Internment Camp, 1948
Highlight: **Golda Meir** visited the Cyprus Detention Camp
The ship **AF Al PI CHEN** is in the Haifa Museum
A Russian Holocaust survivor,
my father lived in Israel for 10 years.
Exhibited at **The Museum of Jewish Heritage**:
A Living Memorial to the Holocaust
36 Battery Park, NYC

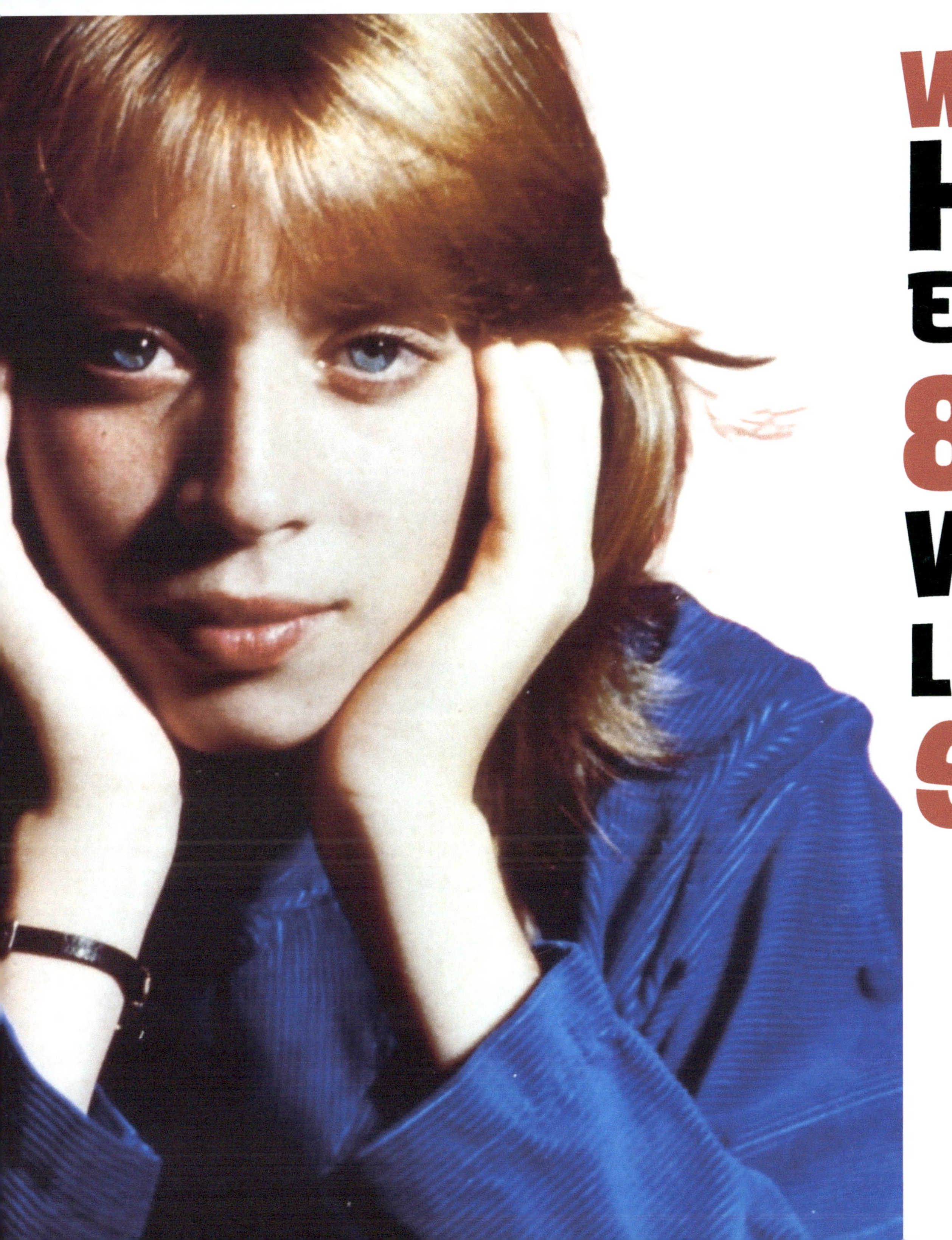

WORLD PEACE
HAPPENS
EVERY DAY FOR
8 HOURS
When Every
Living Being Is
SLEEPING

Sharon Esther Lampert
PRINCESS KADIMAH
8TH PROPHETESS OF ISRAEL
AM YISRAEL CHAI

Published 80+ Books

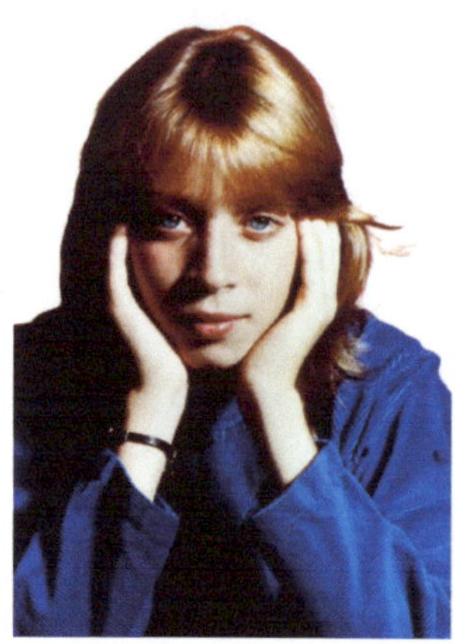

GENIUS: THE GIFT OF DIVINE REVELATION

MY BOOKS WRITE THEMSELVES

I Am Mortal
MY BOOKS ARE IMMORTAL
Please Handle My Books Gently
My Books Are My Remains

Part 1.   World Famous Quotes 2010 — 2025
Part 2.   Format Book: January 2025
Part 3.   Publish: February 2025

Sharon Esther Lampert

SEE THE WORLD THROUGH THE EYES OF A CREATIVE GENIUS
Prodigy, Prophet, Philosopher, Poet, Peacemaker, Paladin of Education, Physicist, Princess

FANS@SharonEstherLampert.com